CREATION

Thirteen 6—in—1
Comprehensive Curriculum Lessons
Grades 1—4

Bible Study, Science, Math, Language Arts, Spelling and Art with 12 "Character, Connections"

Wisdom, Faith, Purity, Responsibility, Diligence, Honesty, Cooperation, Peaceableness, Kindness, Respect, Obedience, Thankfulness

written by
Mary A. Hake

illustrated by
David and Helen Haidle

Master Books®
A Division of New Leaf Publishing Group
www.masterbooks.net

Creation

Thirteen 6-in-1 Comprehensive Curriculum Lessons

First printing: April 2009

ISBN-13: 978-0-89051-566-2
ISBN-10: 0-89051-566-2
Library of Congress Control Number: 2009923584

Interior Design and Layout: David Haidle
Cover Design: Diana Bogardus
Cover Illustrations: David Haidle

Printed in the United States of America

For information regarding author interviews, please contact the publicity department at:
(870) 438-5288.

Please visit our Web site for other great titles:
www.masterbooks.net

All Scripture is from the King James Version of the Bible, unless otherwise noted.

Photo Credits
All images are Shutterstock unless otherwise noted.
clipart.com: 30, 52, 86, 94, 100, 104, 111, 117, 119, 121, 124, 125
http://www.iowas.co.uk/fish%20anatomy.html: 72
NASA: 26, 28
Wikipedia: 79

CREATION

Thirteen 6—in—1
Comprehensive Curriculum Lessons
Grades 1—4

written by
Mary A. Hake

illustrated by
David and Helen Haidle

Master Books®
A Division of New Leaf Publishing Group
www.masterbooks.net

Introduction for Parents & Teachers

Dear Parents and Teachers,

This CREATION curriculum is designed to enrich and expand your regular school material by building on the foundation of God's Creation and exploring it through math, language arts, science, art, and spelling. Each of the first 12 lessons focuses on a day or item of Creation, such as Light, Land, and Animals, along with to a Celebration of Creation lesson and a concluding bonus lesson on God's continuing plan. If you wish to expand the scope of each lesson, you can also use the picture book, *The Creation Story for Children*, as an additional option where noted.

These lessons are designed for grades one through four, but they can be adapted and expanded to include other levels. This curriculum can be used with a single student or with a group, including multiple ages. Feel free to modify it to fit your needs. You may wish to take a Creation Study day every so often, covering an entire Creation lesson instead of regular schoolwork that day — a Creation immersion approach. Or you may desire to spread a lesson over an entire school week. There is no one right way to use this material — do what works best for you. Follow the interest of your child. Experiment, explore, enjoy.

Lessons 1–12 begin with an Introduction that discusses the Scriptural background, followed by an Object Lesson about the topic. At the end of these lessons is a "Character Connection" that relates a particular trait, such as Wisdom, Responsibility, and Kindness, to the lesson and to life. Each of these virtues has a Scripture Search with Bible verses about that trait. You can look up one, some, or all — maybe read one a day or hunt for more verses. This is an optional activity related to the character quality and a practical reminder round out the connection.

Hands–on activities are included throughout this curriculum, as well as extra activities you may wish to incorporate. Some websites appropriate for primary-grade children are listed as sources for additional material on various subjects at the following website: www.masterbooks.org

They are organized by lesson number and in the same order of the lessons in the book. When you see this icon, you will need to go to the website to find the link for that related material.

These sites have been checked to make sure they do not contain objectionable material or annoying advertising. I spent countless hours investigating educational websites in order to choose those most helpful and easy to use

When Bible verse references are given, you may find them in the Bible version(s) you prefer or check more than one for comparison. This is an opportunity to encourage your child to look up verses too. No memory verses have been listed for these sessions. You may wish to choose a verse (or portion of one) from that day's background Scripture to commit to memory or to memorize all of Genesis 1 (through Genesis 2:3) during these CREATION lessons.

While studying academic subjects, it's natural to make biblical and spiritual connections, as we do in this CREATION study. May this course be a starting place for further exploration of God's wonderful Creation. I hope it prompts you and your students to want to learn more, to speak often about God's Creation, and to more fully enjoy the wonderful world in which we live.

—Mary A. Hake, author

CREATION
Curriculum Lessons: Scope & Sequence
Bible, Language, Science, Math, Spelling & Art

Character Connection in Lesson 1 – 12 (Character Traits)

Wisdom, Faith, Purity, Responsibility, Diligence, Honesty, Cooperation, Peaceableness, Kindness, Respect, Obedience, Thankfulness

Suggested Teaching Schedules

These lessons are adaptable for many different schedules. The lessons can last for as little as three weeks or as long as three months. Suggested time frames are listed below. Use the parts of the lessons best suited for your children.

FOUR-WEEK Study of CREATION — One lesson on three or four days each week
SIX-WEEK Study of CREATION — One lesson on two or three days each week
THIRTEEN-WEEK Study of CREATION — One lesson per week for 13 weeks
TWELVE WEEKS of "Character Connections" — One lesson per week for 12 weeks

"The Seven Days of Creation" by Helen Haidle

Sing to the TUNE of "The 12 Days of CHRISTMAS"

On the **FIRST** day of creation, the good Lord gave to me:
    A great light to light the world.

On the **SECOND** day of creation, the good Lord gave to me:
    Clouds and the sky, and great light to light the world.

On the **THIRD** day of creation, the good Lord gave to me:
    Dry land and plants, clouds and the sky, and great light to light the world.

On the **FOURTH** day of creation, the good Lord gave to me:
    Sun, moon, and stars, dry land and plants, clouds and the sky, and great
    light to light the world.

On the **FIFTH** day of creation, the good Lord gave to me:
    Lots of fish and birds, sun, moon, and stars, dry land and plants,
    clouds and the sky, and great light to light the world.

On the **SIXTH** day of creation, the good Lord gave to me:
    Animals and people, lots of fish and birds, sun, moon, and stars,
    dry land and plants, clouds and the sky, and great light to light the world.

On the **SEVENTH** day of creation, the good Lord took a rest.
    What had been created? Animals and people, lots of fish and birds,
    sun, moon, and stars, dry land and plants, clouds and the sky,
    and great light to light the world.

Getting to know David & Helen Haidle

- Freelance writer/editor (Helen) 20 years; and illustrator, fine artist (David) 38 years

- Written and Illustrated 47 books, such as bestsellers: *What Would Jesus Do?, The Candymaker's Gift, CREATION, The Lord is My Shepherd, A Pocket Full of Promises, The Real 12 Days,* with sales of over 1,700,000

- Winners of three C. S. Lewis Awards, and three CBA Silver Medallions

- Speakers and workshop leaders for Oregon Christian Writers Conferences

- Speakers and workshop leaders at Homeschool Conferences in Oregon, Washington, Idaho, and California, and at many Christian schools

- Haidle's publishing company SEED FAITH BOOKS (www.seedfaithbooks.com) publishes Bible resources, especially for Psalm 23 and Creation

- Their non–profit ministry HEART GIFTS gives thousands of books to needy children and adults in detention centers, prisons, foster care, shelters, etc.

Getting to know Mary A. Hake

- Freelance writer 25+ years and freelance editor 12+ years with several publishers.

- President of Oregon Christian Writers; member 23 years

- Christian education teacher 30+ years, Bible study leader and Speaker for women's groups, writer's groups, and homeschool groups

- Contributor to nine books: *Walking with Jesus, Life Savors for Women, His Forever, Living the Serenity Prayer, Seasons of a Woman's Heart, The Gift of Prayer, Hello Future!,* and *Life's Simple Guide to God*

- Writer of hundreds of published nonfiction articles, stories, poems, devotions, puzzles, activities, and newsletters for adults and children

- Associate's Degree in Journalism and Mass Communications

- Chair of Wagner Community Library Advisory Board, Falls City, OR

- Married 35 years to Ted, with two grown daughters, both teachers, whom Mary homeschooled 10 years

Visit Mary's website at www.maryhake.com

God Creates Light

Materials Needed:

☐ **INTRODUCTION:** Bible(s)
☐ **OBJECT LESSON:**
Large cardboard box, sealed shut
Flashlight, dark room
☐ **MATH CONNECTION**
Large rubber band
Paper strip 2-4" wide by 2 feet long
Scotch tape
Optional — Computer and Internet
☐ **ENGLISH/WORD WORK**
Bible or Bible storybook
Paper and pencil, crayons, markers or highlighters
☐ **SCIENCE SCENE**
Objects recognizable by their shapes
Bright light or flashlight, yellow objects
Screen or solid-backed chair
Optional — Computer and Internet
☐ **ART ACTIVITY**
Black construction paper
Black crayon or marker
Newspaper or plastic to cover table
Yellow paint, Craft stick
Optional — Computer and Internet
☐ **SPELLING SPREE**
Paper and pencil
☐ **CONCLUSION:**
Bible, *The Creation Story for Children* book (optional)

"In the beginning, God created the heaven and the earth. . . .
God said, Let there be light . . .
God separated the light from the darkness.
God called the light Day, and the darkness he called Night.
And the evening and the morning were the first day"
(Genesis 1:1, 3–5 KJV).

Lesson Introduction

Materials Needed:
Bible(s)

Read Genesis 1:1–5 together. Discuss any unfamiliar words, such as formless. Talk about what it means to BEGIN something:

God began time. What would it be like if we lived without time?
(Imagine and discuss possibilities.)

Before God created anything, there was no form and no light in what we call the universe. It was just empty nothingness.

Object Lesson

Materials Needed:
Flashlight
Dark room
Large cardboard box, sealed shut, with holes cut as described below.

On one side of the box cut an opening just big enough for a child to insert an arm. The box should be big enough so the sides can't be touched when reaching through the hole. Across from this opening, poke a little hole about the size of this O.

First, have child look into the dark box. **What can you see?** (Nothing, air, cold. Accept and discuss all answers.)

Dark emptiness was all that existed before God created the world. What did God create first? (Light)

- Go into a dark room or closet with the box and a flashlight.

- Hold the box with the opening facing you and the pinprick hole toward the child.

- Point the flashlight into the box. Turn it on.

- Observe how light shines through the tiny hole and lights up a dark place.

- Now remove the flashlight from the box and shine it on the wall, ceiling, floor, etc.

1. Observe the light made by the flashlight.
   Can you see circles in the light? Does part of it seem brighter? (Yes) **Within the light, part seems darker. The light we can see in our world changes — it gets brighter and dimmer.**

2. Discuss your observations of light. (Helps us see color, etc.)

3. Discuss God as light.
- **The Bible says, "… God is light, and in him is no darkness at all"** (1 John 1:5).

God is pure light, and He exists in light brighter than anyone has ever seen.

The first thing God created shows us what He is — LIGHT!

- **James 1:17 tells us God is the Father of all light, with no changing or shadow of turning. His brightness remains the same for all eternity.**

- **Jesus said, "I am the light of the world. Whoever follows me will never walk in darkness, but will have the light of life"** (John 8:12 NIV).

How are you letting Jesus shine in your life right now? (Discuss.)

Math Connection

Materials Needed:
Paper and pencil
Large rubber band
Paper strip 2-4 inches wide by 2 feet long
Scotch tape
Computer and Internet, optional

Infinite means "unmeasurable."
(Discuss infinity—it has no end.)

Let's see how high you can count.
When child tires of counting by 1s, continue counting by 10s, 100s, 1000s, etc., as appropriate by age.

When you can no longer continue, explain:

Numbers go on forever, even if we can't count that high or we don't know the names of such big numbers. You could write the number 1 and keep adding zeroes behind it until you crossed the room, until you went down the sidewalk, and down the street, and to Grandma's house, and across the ocean, and to the moon, and clear to heaven if you could. But you would never reach infinity.

- Draw a big circle.
- Draw another circle just inside that one.
- Keep drawing smaller and smaller circles inside each until you can no longer draw one. If you could keep drawing circles smaller and smaller (and larger and larger), that would show infinity.

Examine a large rubber band.
Where does the rubber band begin?
Does it have an end? (No)

Place forefingers from each hand inside the rubber band and make it go in circles. Explain that this can symbolize infinity or eternity.

On the long, narrow strip of paper, have child write a row of 1s across the paper on both sides.
Tape the strip's ends together to form a circle—a never-ending circle of ones.
Examine both sides.
See how the ones continue around and around.

Visit this link for websites offering more Math Connection suggested activities:

www.masterbooks.org

- Separate the taped ends, and flip one side of the strip over.
- Now tape the back of that side to the front of the other side to make a *mobius strip*.
- Examine the properties of this unending form. It appears to have only one side.
- Draw a line along the middle of the strip.

What happens when you draw a line down the middle? *See website suggestions* (You end where you began—it forms one continuous line.)

Where did numbers come from? (God created numbers.)

Where do you find numbers? (List as many places as you can think of.)

Look around the house, neighborhood, town, etc., for numbers. Be observant all week. See how many places you can list. (Examples: speedometer, house numbers, clocks, magazines, envelopes, …)

Optional Activity:
Count all the 1s you find in your house.

Materials Needed:
Bible or Bible storybook
Paper and pencil
Crayons, markers, or highlighters

A noun (like LIGHT)
   names a person, a place, or a thing.

A verb (like SHINES)
   shows action or the state of being.

1. In your Bible or a Bible storybook, find all the nouns and verbs in Genesis chapter 1.

2. Make two columns, and list the nouns and the verbs.

3. For the words that repeat, keep track of how many times each one is used.

4. Print your Memory Passage or a section of Scripture.

5. Use different color highlighters, markers, or crayons to mark the nouns and verbs.

Extra activity:
Write a story about light, shadows, creation, or whatever this lesson inspires. You could also illustrate it or make a picture book.

Science Scene

Materials Needed:
Objects recognizable by their shapes
Bright light; flashlight
Screen or solid-backed chair
Yellow objects, optional
Computer and Internet, optional

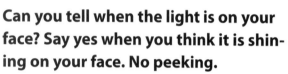

- Have child close his/her eyes.
- Shine a flashlight toward his/her face and then away.

Can you tell when the light is on your face? Say yes when you think it is shining on your face. No peeking.
- Switch roles if desired.

Shadow play:
1. Behind a box, high-backed chair, or screen, gather objects recognizable by their shapes.
2. Shine a bright light toward the wall behind the screen so the child can see the light above the screen.
3. Hold each object in front of the light so its shadow is projected onto the wall. Have child guess what made the shadow.

God Creates Light

Ask: **If there was no light, would we see shadows? Why or why not?**
Turn off the light and hold up an object behind the screen.

Do you see a shadow? (no)
Let's make up our own hand shadows.

Demonstrate.
Show illustrations of hand shadow forms to copy. See these websites in the box at the bottom of the page for ideas.

Experiment.
1. Have child shine a light on something to create a shadow.
2. Observe the size and direction of the shadow.
3. Move the light closer and farther away; shine it down from above and up from below.
4. Notice how the direction and nearness of the light source make shadows get taller or smaller.
5. Record observations.

Want to see more shadow puppet activities and videos? Go to this website for links:

www.masterbooks.org

12

Nighttime Experiment:
Go outside after dark
with a flashlight.
Shine the flashlight
all around the area

where you are standing.
Watch where the light lands. Now shine the
flashlight up into the dark sky.
**You cannot see the light's path for
very far, but the light keeps going up
to outer space. Light travels on and on
forever.**

Optional Activity:
- Make a collection of yellow objects
  that remind you of light.

- Look at these objects in the dark.

Can you see their color when it's dark?

- Turn on the light.

The color returns when there is light.

We need light to see colors.

- Look at a picture of the USA at night.

For Older Children:
Talk about how far light travels in one
second, in one minute, in one hour, and in
one year. You may want to have the student look up this information.

**Light travels about 186,000 miles per
second.** (Actually, about 186,282.397
miles—these numbers are rounded.)
1. Multiply 186,000 by 60 to find out the
   miles light travels in one minute.
   (11,160,000 miles per minute)
2. Multiply this by 60 to find out the miles
   light travels in one hour.
   (669,600,000 miles per hour)
3. Multiply this by 24 to find out the miles
   light travels in one day.
   (1,607,040,000 miles per day)
4. Multiply this by 365 to find out how far
   light travels in one year.

**A light year is 5,865,696,000,000 miles.
That's almost six trillion miles!**
(or 9,460,800,000,000 kilometers)

**A light nanosecond is the distance light
can travel in a billionth of a
second, about one foot** (or 30 cm).

5. To see a demonstration of how fast
   light travels in one second.

**It's hard to imagine how fast light can actually travel in one second.
To see a demonstration of this and a picture of the USA at night,
visit our site at:**
www.masterbooks.org

Art Activity

Materials Needed:
Black construction paper
Black crayon or marker
Newspaper or plastic to cover table
Yellow paint, craft stick, optional
Computer and Internet, optional

- On black construction paper, have child use a black crayon or marker to make 1s all over the page.
- Hold up the finished page a few yards from child.

Black on black does not show up well, does it?

- Have child place the black paper on a newspaper- or plastic-covered surface.
- Pour a small bit of yellow paint in the middle of the black page.
- With a finger or a craft stick, from the center of the paint spread out rays—like 1s spreading from the bright blob in all directions.
- Allow to dry.

(The art activities may be collected from each lesson to put together in a binder.)

Extra activity:
Make pictures with a virtual Lite Brite online. Experiment with designs.

Spelling Spree

Materials Needed:
Paper and pencil

1. Choose words appropriate for the child's grade level/ability from the memory passage and/or found in any other subject in this Creation lesson.

Examples: God, creation, create, light, dark, night, black, shadow, travel, etc. (This can be done by the teacher or with the child.)

2. Have child read the list to you, pronouncing each word correctly and spelling it aloud.

3. Have child copy the spelling words and define each one.

4. Child may find or draw a picture to illustrate each word.

5. Child may use each word in a sentence or write a story containing the spelling words.

Suggestion: Give a spelling test on the words at the end of the week.

Conclusion

Materials Needed:
Bible,
The Creation Story for Children (optional)

Close the day's study by reviewing the Bible verses listed on page 8.

(If you choose to incorporate _The Creation Story for Children_, read to the end of the account of Day One.)

Read 2 Corinthians 4:6.
God created light to brighten the darkness.

God sent Jesus to Earth to bring His light to people so they could know God.

Aren't you glad God has shined His light into our hearts and helped us know Him? Let's thank God for light that shines in our world and for Jesus Who shines in our hearts.

For Older Students:
Research what happens when light shines through a prism.

For Older Students:
Read John 8:12 — Jesus said, "I am the light of the world. He who follows Me shall not walk in darkness, but have the light of life." **In what way would someone "walk in darkness" even if he or she is not blind?**

What does walking in "darkness" mean?
(To live life without knowing God.)

How do you think Jesus gives us "light"?
(Jesus doesn't shine a bright light on us. But He "opens the eyes of our heart" and helps us "see" who we are. Jesus helps us see who God is. Jesus helps us "see" what we should do and how God wants us to live. With Jesus in our lives, we can "walk in the light" because we live with God every day.)

Let's thank God for light that shines in our world and for Jesus who shines in our hearts.

Interested in prisms? See what happens when light shines through a prism when you visit links on the following webpage:
www.masterbooks.org

Lesson 1

Character Connection

All wisdom comes from God.

Scripture Search

Exodus 31:3	1 Kings 4:29–30
Job 28:28	Psalm 111:10
Proverbs 2:6	Proverbs 4:5–11
Isaiah 11:2	Matthew 7:24–25
2 Timothy 3:15	James 3:17–18

What is wisdom? (Discuss.)

Wisdom means knowing how to use what you know in the best way.

A wise person understands things.

A wise person knows what is right.

A wise person comes up with a good solution to a problem.

Example: *Suppose you can choose a new book as a prize. Your little brother and sister would really like a book too, but they didn't win one.*

You would really like to read a mystery book. Instead, you choose a book about nature that you can read to your brother and sister.

That way you all enjoy the book together and read it again and again. You also learn cool new facts about God's creation.

- **You made a wise decision when you chose the book about nature.**

Materials Needed:
Bible(s)

A small **W** cut from paper, clear tape

For Optional Activity:
Computer with Internet, optional
Heavy paper, pencil, marker, scissors

Wisdom

Why would it take great wisdom to create the whole universe, to make everything from nothing? (Discuss.)

Think about the wisdom God showed in making the Earth and everything on it as a home for His creatures.

Think about the wisdom it took to design the human body, with all its many parts.

**God made everything very good — to work the way He planned.
God's mighty wisdom is shown in His Creation.**

And God wants us to be wise too.

Other Thoughts on WISDOM:

- **We can ask our Heavenly Father, and He will give us the wisdom we need.** See James 1:5 and Psalm 98:12.

- **The Bible says the wise person will be happy** (Proverbs 3:13).

- **The Bible says teaching a wise person will make him wiser** (Proverbs 9:9).

- **God's Word will teach us wisdom. We should be like Jesus, who grew in wisdom** (Luke 2:40).

Optional Activity:
A simple craft to emphasize the importance of knowing God's Word, which makes us wise.

For Closing Discussion:

How can you tell someone is wise? (The person makes smart choices, thinks before acting, tries to understand others, learns from mistakes, works out problems so as not to hurt others, says no to dangerous things, tries to learn something new each day, plans ahead, listens to others, etc.)

When have you showed wisdom? (Encourage personal sharing.)

How can you act wisely today? (Encourage personal sharing.)

WISDOM Reminder:
Tape a **W** for Wisdom to your clock and/or watch to remind you to seek wisdom. Colossians 4:5 (KJV) says, "Walk in wisdom … redeeming the time."

It's always the right time to practice wisdom.

Visit this link for websites offering simple crafts emphasizing the importance of knowing God's Word:

www.masterbooks.org

Lesson 2

God Creates Sky

Materials Needed:

☐ **INTRODUCTION:** Bible(s)
☐ **OBJECT LESSON:**
Large clear plastic container or dishpan
Smaller clear container with lid
Water, towel, Bible
☐ **MATH CONNECTION**
Paper and pencil
Blue crayon or blue marker
"Snowflake" stamps from 2006, optional
Snowflake worksheet copied
Optional — Computer and Internet
☐ **ENGLISH/WORD WORK**
Paper and pencil
☐ **SCIENCE SCENE**
Paper and pencil
Optional — Computer and Internet
☐ **ART ACTIVITY**
Small sponges cut into cloud shapes
Blue construction paper
White (tempera) paint
  For #2:
White construction paper
White crayon
Blue watercolor paint and brush
Optional — Computer and Internet
☐ **SPELLING SPREE**
Paper and pencil
☐ **CONCLUSION:**
Bible, *The Creation Story for Children Book* (optional)

God said, Let there be a firmament in the midst of the waters, and let it divide the waters from the waters . . . . and it was so. . . And the evening and the morning were the second day" (Genesis 1:6–8 KJV).

Lesson Introduction

Materials Needed:
Bible(s)

Read Genesis 1:6–8 together.
Discuss any unfamiliar words.
Talk about the sky and how high it goes.

Let child share thoughts.

Have you ever been up in the sky (in an airplane, hot air balloon, etc.)**?**
How do things look from up high?

Go outdoors and observe the sky. If there are clouds, observe their shapes and colors.

Do you see the clouds moving?
Do you see how they change shapes?
What makes the clouds move across the sky? (Wind)

Object Lesson

Materials Needed:
Large clear plastic container or dishpan
Smaller clear container with lid
Water, towel, Bible

Fill a large clear plastic container (Tupperware works well for this) or dishpan with water deep enough to cover the smaller container. Take the smaller clear plastic container with its lid tightly sealed, and place in the water.

Why does this container float?
(It is full of air, and air weighs less than water.)
Push down on the small container. Feel the push of the water against it. Hold the smaller container submersed in the water, but not touching the bottom.

See how the water is divided by the container full of air. Some water is above the container, and some water is below it. The container is surrounded by water, but there is no water inside it.

Remove the small container and dry it off. Open the lid and let the child feel inside. Observe that it stayed dry inside even when underwater.

God divided the waters above, in the sky, from the waters below, on the earth.

God filled in the space between the waters with air. We call this huge space "sky." (Child may draw a picture of this.)

The Bible talks about the sky in many places. Read and discuss the following Bible verses about weather.

1. **The first rain fell from the sky when God sent the flood**.
   Genesis 7:11–12; 8:2.
2. **Before that a mist watered the earth.** Genesis 2:6.
3. **Sometimes God sends hail and lightning from the sky**.
   Exodus 9:22–23; 2 Samuel 22:10–14.
4. **God controls the weather**. Psalm 147:8, 16–17; Job 37:3–6.
5. **Jesus said people could tell what the weather would be by watching the sky**. Matthew 16:2–3a.

Check the sky in the morning and evening for a few days. See if you can predict nice or bad weather.

Math Connection

Materials Needed:

Paper and pencil

Blue crayon or blue marker

"Snowflake" stamps, stickers or cutouts, optional

Make a snowflake worksheet

Computer and Internet, optional

1. On a plain piece of paper, have child draw water drops all over the page.
2. Next, draw a cloud circle around each group of ten raindrops.
3. Leave the leftover drops (less than ten raindrops) outside the cloud circles.
4. Have child count the groups of ten.

Form a chart like this to record the total:

One ten = _____ (10).

Two tens = _____ (20).

Three tens = _____ (30).

Ten tens = _____ (100).

5. Have child count the raindrops and fill in the totals on the chart.

First, count the ones in the clouds by tens. (Each cloud has ten drops.)

Total raindrops in clouds _____

Plus the single drops leftover   + _____

Equals the final total   _____

(Count each drop to check the answer.)

6. Use the snowflake postage stamps or your snowflake worksheet for counting, adding, multiplying, matching, and creating sequences.

- SORT snowflakes by shape.
- COUNT the total of each snowflake shape and record these.
- ADD the totals to find our how many snowflakes all together.

7. Make repeating patterns, then have child point to, draw, or find a picture of what would come next.

Example:

Which shape comes next? Continue repeating the pattern across the page.

Download a sheet of snowflake designs, as well as where you can go to download a PDF of numbered snowflakes (0-20). Hint: You can also learn more about compound words through links at the website that will help prepare for English Word Work on the following page:

www.masterbooks.org

English Word Work

Materials Needed:

Paper and pencil

Computer and Internet, optional

Search to find words within words.

Example: Firmament contains the word "firm."

It also contains the words "ma" and "me."

Divide these words to find a new word.

(Some words contain more than one word.)

Cloud (loud)

Lightning (light)

Earth (ear, art)

Weather (eat, her)

Praise (raise)

Wonderful (won, on, wonder)

Evening (eve, even)

Below (be, low)

Today (to, day)

Snowflake (snow, no, now, flake, lake)

Some words are formed by joining two words to make one compound word.

How many compound words can you list? Here are some to get you started.

Draw a line to separate the two smaller words that make each compound word.

skylight   (sky/light)

daytime

nightfall

rainbow

waterfall

windmill

snowflake

Materials Needed:

Paper and pencil
Computer and Internet, optional

Talk about how the weather changes.
List all the types of weather you can.

Fill in the answers in this weather poem.
(Read aloud or copy the poem so child can
write in the answers.)

1. **Overhead the blue seems near
   Every way you look from here,
   And no clouds today appear,
   So we say the sky is _____.**
   (clear)

2. **Sometimes clouds are white and
   fluffy;
   Other clouds look dark and huffy.
   Many drops they do contain,
   Until they send drops down as
   _____.** (rain)

3. **We may not see this passing by,
   But it helps the kites to fly.
   Sometimes blowing very strong,
   _____ works to move the clouds
   along.** (wind)

4. **Down falls white onto the ground,
   Quietly, without much sound.
   Soon white covers all below.**

We enjoy the winter's _____.
(snow)

5. **When ice forms into hard balls,
   And from the sky above it falls,
   It can sound like pounding nails.
   That's what happens when it _____.**
   (hails)

Do you wonder why the sky is blue? This
activity shows why.
Clouds are made up of water and little
bits of dust or smoke that collect in the
sky.
The three main types of clouds are:

1. **Cirrus clouds — high and wispy;**
2. **Cumulous clouds — large and fluffy;**
3. **Stratus clouds — low and stretched
   across the sky. (Fog is made of low
   stratus clouds.)**

**Watch for these different types of
clouds in the sky. Which kind of clouds
have you seen the most?
What kind of clouds do you see outside
today?**

You may want to record which clouds
you see each day.

Find a quick and easy experiment to learn why the sky is blue:
www.masterbooks.org

Science Scene, *continued*

Learn more about weather by visiting our website for links to learn about building a fog chamber, making a cloud in a bottle, or just to learn more in general clouds or weather through additional lessons, songs, and games:

www.masterbooks.org

Art Activity

Materials Needed:
Small sponges cut into cloud shapes
Blue construction paper
White (tempera) paint

Materials Needed for #2:
White construction paper
White crayon
Blue watercolor paint and brush

Following are two ways to create cloud pictures:

Version 1:
- Dip cloud-shaped sponges in white tempera paint.
- Gently shake off excess paint.
- Blot onto blue construction paper to form clouds.
- Allow to dry.

Version 2:
- Color white clouds with white crayons on white construction paper.
- With blue watercolor paint, cover the paper with a light coat.
- The white clouds will show through.
- Allow to dry.

Extra Activities

(The art activities may be collected from each lesson to put together in a book or binder. You may wish to write the day of creation on the picture.)

Two carved bars of Ivory Snow soap:

A snail shell snow sculpture:

Get instructions for how to draw and paint a snow scene, carving a snow sculpture from soap, making a wind spiral or a wind chime:

www.masterbooks.org

Spelling Spree

Materials Needed:
Paper and pencil
Scrambled spelling words

Choose words appropriate for the child's grade level/ability from this Creation lesson. (This can be done by the teacher or with the child.)

Examples: sky, clouds, rain, wind, snow, oxygen, weather, snowflakes, raindrops, etc.

You might want to use some compound words on your list.

Have child read the list to you, pronouncing each word correctly and spelling it aloud. Make sure child knows the meaning of each word.

Form scrambled words by mixing up the letters in each word for your student to unscramble.

Example:	redhunt	= thunder
	doucls	= clouds
	gexyno	= oxygen
	nosw	= snow
	rustrat	= stratus
	nari	= rain
	nidw	= wind

Give a spelling test on the words at the end of the week.

Conclusion

Materials Needed:
Bible
The Creation Story for Children (optional)

If you choose to incorporate *The Creation Story for Children*, (optional) read to the end of the account of Day Two.

Discuss how things changed from Day One to Day Two.

Extra activity:
Take time during the day or in the evening to lie down outside on the grass and look at the big sky overhead.

Read Psalm 104:11 & 12.
"For as the heavens are high above the earth, so great is His mercy towards those who fear Him; As far as the east is from the west, so far has He removed our transgressions from us" (NKJV).

Talk about how the great big sky can remind us of God's great love that surrounds us.

2

Lesson

Materials Needed:
Bible(s)
Heavyweight paper and scissors or
Plastic eyeglass frames
Blue cellophane
Tape or glue
For Optional Activity:
Ingredients for making cookies or a cake measured into containers, and tools needed for recipe, optional (Don't let the pans be seen until you're ready.)

Faith

Do you believe in things you can't see?
(Discuss. Think about our digestive system, our brain, the blood running through our veins, the vast universe, etc.)

You can't see your brain, but you know you have one.
Your brain can think, and your brain tells your body how to work.

You can't see the sun at night or when storm clouds cover the sky, but you know the sun is there and it is still shining.

Believing what you can't see shows FAITH.

By faith, we believe in God and we believe God loves us.

We believe God created the world.
We believe God made light shine in the darkness and God made the sky.

Even though we can't see God, we know God is real.

Faith helps us believe in God and in the Truth of His Word.

Scripture Search
Hebrews 11:1, 3	Mark 9:23
Romans 1:17	Romans 10:17
2 Corinthians 5:7	Ephesians 6:16
2 Timothy 3:15	Hebrews 10:23
Hebrews 12:2	

The Bible says without faith it is impossible to please God (Hebrews 11:6).

God's people love God and want to please Him. We please God when we trust His love and His care.

Faith believes that God is Who He says He is and that God does what He says He will do.

When we pray and ask God for help, we know God will do what is best.
This shows faith in God and in His care for us.

Extra activity:
Set out the ingredients for baking cookies or a cake.

As you add each ingredient to the mixing bowl, have child taste it. (Flour, sugar, salt, vanilla, etc. Do not taste raw eggs.)

Explain: **Some ingredients taste good alone, but some do not taste good by themselves.** Have child help stir the batter.

Do you have faith these ingredients will turn into a tasty treat to eat?
(Accept any answer)
Bake the cookies or cake, then enjoy.

This treat is the proof of our "faith" that the batter we mixed would turn into something good.

Faith doesn't have to see something in order to believe it is true.

For Closing Discussion:
Think about times you have shown faith. (Encourage personal sharing)
How can you put faith into practice every day? (Pray and believe God will answer, trust your parents and teachers, read and believe God's Word, obey those in charge, have faith — trust that your good behavior will be rewarded)

FAITH Reminder:
Cut out an eyeglasses shape from heavy paper or use old plastic frames.
Add lenses of blue cellophane.
Tape or glue them to the eyeglass frames.
Let your child wear them for a while.

Discuss:
How does looking through blue-sky lenses remind you to look at life and its events with eyes of faith? (We can trust God's promises no matter how bad things look at the moment. God wants us to look at life through eyes of faith)

Remember to see things with your eyes of faith and not only by sight.

Lesson 3

"And God said, Let the waters under the heaven be gathered together unto one place . . . and the gathering together of the waters called he Seas: and God saw that it was good" (Genesis 1:9–10 KJV).

Materials Needed:

☐ **INTRODUCTION:** Bible(s)
Pictures of various forms of water (ocean, river, lake, stream, puddle, waterfall, glacier, iceberg, etc.)

☐ **OBJECT LESSON:**
Ice cubes, ice cube tray, pan, cup
Heat source (kitchen stove)

☐ **MATH CONNECTION**
Teaspoon, tablespoon, 1-cup measuring cup. Pint, quart, and gallon jars or containers. Gallon pitcher and Ruler, optional

☐ **ENGLISH/WORD WORK**
Paper and pencil

☐ **SCIENCE SCENE**
Metal spoon,
Teakettle to heat, filled with water
Oven mitt
Computer and Internet, optional

☐ **ART ACTIVITY**
Heavy paper or cardstock,
Colored construction paper, scissors, glue
Computer and Internet, optional

☐ **SPELLING SPREE**
Paper, watercolors
Thin-tipped paintbrush

☐ **CONCLUSION:**
The Creation Story for Children book (optional), Bible

Lesson Introduction

Materials Needed: Bible(s)
Pictures of various forms of water (ocean, river, lake, stream, puddle, waterfall, glacier, iceberg, etc.)

Read Genesis 1:9–10 together. Discuss any unfamiliar words.
Where is water found on Earth? (Oceans, rivers, lakes, streams, puddles, underground, etc.)
God created the waters. On Day Three, God placed the water in assigned places.

Talk about bodies of water you have seen. Show photos or find pictures in magazines, books, or online of various types of water, including waterfalls and the ocean.
Discuss how the power of water reminds us of the power or God, our Creator.
Read Psalm 33:7, Psalm 89:9, Psalm 93:3–4, and Psalm 96:11.

Object Lesson

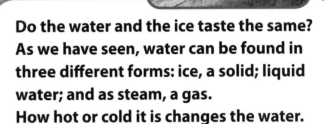

Materials Needed:
Ice cubes
Ice cube tray
Pan and a cup
Heat source (kitchen stove)

Hold up some ice cubes.
What are these? (Ice cubes)
What is ice made of? (If child doesn't answer water, don't tell.)
Let's see what will happen when the ice is heated.
Place all but one ice cube in a pan on the stove and turn on the heat.
Have child watch the changes.
Talk about what you observe.

When the ice has melted, pour a little of the water into a cup and set aside.
Leave the rest on the heat to evaporate.
Observe and discuss this process.
Where does the water go when it evaporates? (Into the air)

When the water in the cup has cooled, have child take a drink of it, then taste the ice.

Do the water and the ice taste the same?
As we have seen, water can be found in three different forms: ice, a solid; liquid water; and as steam, a gas.
How hot or cold it is changes the water.

Which form is the coldest? (Ice)
Which form is the hottest? (Steam)
Compare the shapes of these forms of water.
Which one keeps its shape? (Ice)
What shape does liquid water take? (The shape of the container it is in.)

Place water in an ice cube tray in the freezer to observe the reverse process.
Check back later to see and feel the ice.
If you use distilled water, you will see ice spikes form when it freezes.

When you drink ice water, you have two of water's forms at once.
Water is found on Earth in all three forms. We see liquid water every day.
There is hot steam inside the Earth.
There is frozen water on land, like snow and glaciers, and in the oceans there are icebergs.

Visit this link for websites showing pictures of glaciers and icebergs:

www.masterbooks.org

29

Math Connection

Materials Needed:

Teaspoon
Tablespoon
1–cup measuring cup
Pint, quart, and gallon jars or containers
Gallon pitcher, optional
Ruler, optional

Set out the teaspoon, tablespoon, cup, pint, quart, and gallon containers near a sink.

Hold a tablespoon steady and measure teaspoons filled with water into the tablespoon until it is full.
How many teaspoons does it take to make one tablespoon? (Three)
Record this on your paper:
3 teaspoons equal 1 tablespoon.

Repeat this process with each larger container. Measure carefully.
Record each finding.

How many tablespoons does it take to make one cup? (16)

How many cups does it take to make one pint? (Two)

How many pints does it take to make one quart? (Two)

How many quarts does it take to make one gallon? (Four)

**For those who can multiply, figure out other conversions, such as how many cups equal one quart (2 cups x 2 pints).

You can test your answers with the water and containers.

Extra activity:

Measure the water to find out how many gallons you use next time you take a bath.

Fill the tub by first filling a gallon pitcher, then pouring in the water from the pitcher over and over until you have enough water for your bath.

Keep track of how many gallons you use. (You can also use a one-half gallon pitcher and multiply by two to find how many gallons.)

You may also want to measure the depth of the water with a ruler.

English Word Work

Materials Needed:

Paper and pencil

Write a poem about water — any type of water you choose, or as many different forms of water as you wish to include. Poems do not have to rhyme, but they should have a rhythm.
Use words that help others see what you are writing about.
Read the poem aloud to hear its beat.
OR
Write a story about water.

1. You might imagine you are a drop of water and write about your journey from a rain cloud to the ground to the ocean, etc.

2. Or use your imagination to write a fantasy about being lost in the desert and finding water in surprising and interesting or even funny places.

For Older Students:

Write a poem or a story about being on a expedition to the North Pole and exploring an iceberg.

Draw illustrations for your story.

What adventures would you encounter?
What would you discover?

What dangers would threaten your life?

Who would come to your rescue?
Can you think of an ending to your story that would surprise your reader?

Visit this link for a thumbnail image of an iceberg:

www.masterbooks.org

Materials Needed:
Metal spoon
Teakettle to heat, filled with water
Oven mitt
Computer and Internet, optional

1. **Water falls from clouds in the sky as rain, snow, hail, or sleet.**
   This is called PRECIPITATION.

On the ground, water is found in various places, as we named earlier.

Water flows downhill and collects into streams and rivers, which eventually empty into the ocean.

**Include for older children:

2. **Some water soaks into the ground. This is called INFILTRATION. (The water table is the water near the surface of the Earth.)**

3. **Some of the water in lakes and streams and oceans goes back up into the air as water vapor.**

This process is called EVAPORATION.

The water vapor in the air forms clouds.

4. **When the clouds get too heavy, they let drops of water escape as PRECIPITATION, and the cycle starts all over again.**

Learn the steps of the water cycle. (Precipitation, water on earth, evaporation, water vapor forming clouds, and the process repeats over and over).

Follow a drop of water through the steps. Child may draw a picture to show the water cycle.

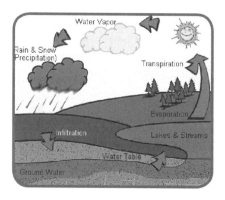

Visit this link for websites offering more information about various bodies of water, the world's longest rivers, photos and information about Niagra Falls, and details of water cycles (Includes a cutout.):

www.masterbooks.org

Water Experiments

1. Place a bowl of water somewhere warm.
    Check it throughout the day/week to see how the water level goes down as the water evaporates. How long does it take for the water to disappear?
    You could measure its depth every few hours and record the changes on a chart.

2. Make your own rain.
    Place a metal spoon in the freezer for 30 minutes.
    Wearing an oven mitt, hold the cold spoon over steam from a boiling teakettle or pan of water. Watch the water drops form on the spoon and then drip from it as "rain."

3. Look at pockets of air trapped in water:
    (See below.)

4. Do hot and cold water mix? Try this experiment:
    (See below.)

Visit this link for websites displaying pockets of air trapped in water and hot and cold water experiments:

www.masterbooks.org

Art Activity

Materials Needed:
Large sheet of heavy paper or cardstock
Colored construction paper
Scissors
Glue

Cut different colors of construction paper into triangles of various sizes. (Teacher or child can cut them out.)

These three-sided shapes remind us this is Day Three of creation.

Arrange the shapes to create pictures.
Glue them onto a large sheet of construction paper or cardstock.

Simple pictures made from Tangrams (geometric shapes of triangles, squares, diamonds, rectangles, etc.) can give ideas for this type of mosaic picture.

(The art activities may be collected from each lesson to put together in a book or binder. You may wish to write the day of creation on the picture.)

Tangram Pattern

Visit this link for websites offering more information about Tangram and the artistic power of shapes:

www.masterbooks.org

34

Spelling Spree

Materials Needed:
Watercolors
Thin-tipped paintbrush
Paper

Choose words appropriate for the child's grade level/ability from this Creation lesson. (This can be done by the teacher or with the child.)
Examples: water, raindrop, cycle, measure, water vapor, evaporation, precipitation, etc.

Have child read the list to you, pronouncing each word correctly and spelling it aloud. Make sure child knows the meaning of each word.

Using watercolors and a thin-tipped paintbrush, have child spell each word with paint. Each word could be a different color.

Give a spelling test on the words at the end of the week.

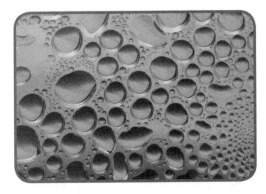

Conclusion

Materials Needed:
The Creation Story for Children (optional)
Paper and pencil

To incorporate *The Creation Story for Children*, review the account of Day Two, with special emphasis on the division of the water above and the water below.

Go on a water watch this week to find as many different places and forms of water as you can. Keep a list of what you find.

Don't waste water. A faucet dripping just one drop a minute will waste 46 gallons in a year. (That would fill your bathtub!)

Be sure to drink plenty of water each day to be healthy. How long do you think you could live without water? (Only three to four days.)

You may want to keep track of how many glasses of water you drink each day.

Thank God for the gift of WATER.

Character Connection

Materials Needed:
Bible(s)
Water bottle
Stick-on label or paper and tape
A marker
For Optional Activity:
Glass jar with lid, water, food color, bleach

Purity

God created everything good and pure.
God made the water pure and clean.
If I put a spoonful of dirt in a glass of water, would you want to drink it?

We like things to be pure.

Would you want salt mixed with your sugar?

Would you like pepper in the cookie dough?

If you add water to the gasoline put in our car, what would happen? (The car wouldn't run.)

If a medicine is not made with pure ingredients, what might happen?

(The medicine could be harmful for our bodies instead of helpful.)

Purity is important for things to work properly.

Just as we like things to be pure, God desires us to be pure. God wants us to do what is right and good. God doesn't want us to do what is wrong.

How can people stay pure? (Discuss)

Everything we see and hear affects us. What happens to things we see? (It goes into our minds, and we remember it.)

If we take in impure things, what will happen to us?
(They can hurt us or harm us in some way.)

Jesus said what is in a person's heart will come out.
To be pure, guard your mind and heart against ungodly things.

Philippians 4:8 tells us to think about things that are true, honest, just, pure, lovely, and good. What "good" things can we think about today?

First Timothy 5:22 says to keep yourself pure. Putting good things into our mind will help keep our thoughts pure.

Scripture Search

Psalm 24:3–5
1 Timothy 1:5; 2
Titus 1:15
1 Peter 1:22

Matthew 5:8
Timothy 2:22
James 3:17

If our thoughts are pure, pure actions should follow. How would a pure person act? (discuss)

Optional Activity

1. Fill a glass jar with water.

This water represents your life.

2. Place one small drop of food color in the water.

When you let an impurity into your life, it can affect your whole life.

3. Put the lid on the jar and gently shake it so the color is distributed throughout.

How can we get rid of the impurity that stains our lives? (Discuss)

When we confess our sins to Jesus and ask Him to take them away, He will. Jesus will forgive us and clean up our lives.

4. Pour some bleach (It may take ¼ cup.) into the jar and replace the lid.

5. Shake the jar, then let it sit, and watch the water turn clear. It may take several minutes.

Let's keep our lives pure and clean.
(Note: Be careful when disposing of the bleach water so it doesn't splash on your clothes. You can pour it down the drain to purify the drainpipe.)

For Closing Discussion

How can being pure make our lives better? (Encourage personal sharing.)

How can you practice purity in your daily life? (Be careful what you read or watch, don't repeat gossip or bad language, pray and ask God to help you, etc.)

PURITY Reminder:

Make a label that says "**Stay PURE**" and put it on your water bottle.

Every time you see these words, determine to keep your life pure.
This acrostic may help guide you.
When you aren't sure if something is OK and good for you,

> **P**lace it
> **U**nder the
> **R**edeemer's
> **E**yes

Is it something Jesus would approve? If not, you should not participate.
Purity pleases God.

Lesson 4

"God said, Let dry ground appear: and it was so. And God called the dry ground Earth . . . and God saw that it was good" (Genesis 1:9–10 KJV).

Materials Needed:

☐ **INTRODUCTION:**
Bible(s), globe or world map

☐ **OBJECT LESSON:**
Dishpan or plastic-lined cardboard box
Sand, water, small shovel or large metal spoon, globe

☐ **MATH CONNECTION**
Paper and pencil

☐ **ENGLISH/WORD WORK**
Paper and pencil

☐ **SCIENCE SCENE**
Pitcher, dry sand or fine, dry soil
Pictures of a sand dune, dust storm, and a glacier, ice cube.
Different types and colors of soil and rocks (or pictures of various types)
Magnifying glass, small scale for weighing rocks, penny, nail
Microscope, optional
Computer and Internet, optional

☐ **ART ACTIVITY**
Clear jar, soil samples of different colors and textures, tiny rocks,
Melted wax, optional

☐ **SPELLING SPREE**
Paper and pencil, heavy paper or cardstock, scissors, marker

☐ **CONCLUSION:**
Bible, *The Creation Story for Children* book (optional)

Lesson Introduction

Materials Needed:
Bible(s)
Globe or world map

Read Genesis 1:9–10.
In our last lesson, we looked at the waters. Today we will talk about the land God created.

Read 2 Peter 3:5b, and discuss what it says.
The Bible tells us the land came out of the water.
Look at a globe or a world map. Name the continents and count them. Notice how water surrounds all the landmasses.

God _spoke_ and created the Heaven and the Earth from nothing.
God _spoke_ and divided the waters.
God _spoke_ and the dry land appeared.
God's word is mighty. What God says happens.

Object Lesson

Materials Needed:
Globe
Dishpan or plastic-lined cardboard box
Small shovel or large metal spoon

Sand — Place at least three inches of sand in the bottom of a dishpan or box.
Water — Add enough water to cover the sand by about one inch.

- **Water once covered the face of the entire Earth.**

- **Then God gathered the waters into one place, and the dry land appeared.**

- **Look at the globe. How much water covers the earth?** (Lots!)

- **Is there more water or more land on our planet?** (Much more water.)

1. With a small shovel or a large metal spoon, dig the sand out from the bottom of the container. Pile it at one end of the pan.

2. Pack the sand so it holds together in a firm mound at one end of the pan.

This mountain of sand reminds us how God called the land to come out of the water on Day Three of Creation.

Optional Discussion:
Why is land important?

(Land provides a place where many creatures can live. Land provides places to walk and to rest. Land provides a place to plant seeds and where food can grow.)

In what ways would our lives change if there was only water on earth and no land?

(Nothing could grow except water plants. Many animals wouldn't have homes or food without land. People couldn't live without land and the plants grown for food. Only sea creatures could live.)

NOTE: Set the pan aside to allow the sand to dry. Use it during the science lesson.

Math Connection

Materials Needed::
Print the alphabet across a piece of paper. Under each letter, write a number, beginning with 1 for A and ending with 26 for Z.

Use the number for each letter in the math problems below.

Have child write the matching numbers below each letter in the words given below.
Example: L   A   N   D
      11   1   14   4

Then add the numbers for each letter together. (11 + 1+ 14 + 4 = 30.)

[EXTRA: If you add the numbers in this sum, 3 + 0, you get 3. Land was formed on the third day of creation.]

Which word's letters total the biggest sum? (Water.)

Which words add to the same total? (Heaven and cloud.)

Which word has the smallest total? (God; He should always come first.)

Answers:

G O D	7 + 15 + 4 = 26
D A Y	4 + 1 + 25 = 30
N I G H T	14 + 9 + 7 + 8 + 20 = 58
F O R M	6 + 15 + 18 + 13 = 62
S K Y	19 + 11 + 25 = 45
C R E A T E	3 + 18 + 5 + 1 + 20 + 5 = 52
L I G H T	12 + 9 + 7 + 8 + 20 = 56
H E A V E N	8 + 5 + 1 + 22 + 5 + 14 = 55
W A T E R	23 + 1 + 20 + 5 + 18 = 67
C L O U D	3 + 12 + 15 + 21 + 4 = 55

G O D	C R E A T E
_ _ _	_ _ _ _ _ _
D A Y	L I G H T
_ _ _	_ _ _ _ _
N I G H T	H E A V E N
_ _ _ - _ _	_ _ _ _ _ _
F O R M	W A T E R
_ _ _ _	_ _ _ _ _
S K Y	C L O U D
_ _ _	_ _ _ _ _

English Word Work

For MORE "MATH FUN":

Try this with your name, your street, your city, and other words.

- **ADD** the totals of different words,
  SKY + CLOUD (100)
  CLOUD + WATER (122)
  SKY + CLOUD + WATER (167).

- **SUBTRACT** one word from another.

For Older Children:

- **MULTIPLY** the letters together instead of adding.

- **DIVIDE** one word by another.

- **Make FRACTIONS** from the words.
  Example: D A Y =   30   (Reduces to 15)
                 NIGHT   58   29

Materials Needed:
Paper and pencil

Verbs are action words.
Think of the things you can do with earth or soil.
List all the verbs that come to mind.
(Examples: measure, haul, pile, etc.)

Write sentences using these words.
Underline the verbs.

For Older Children:
Make some sentences in present tense, some past tense, and some future tense.
Label the tense used in each sentence.
Examples:
I <u>play</u> in the sandbox.
  Present tense
The workmen <u>tunneled</u> into the mountain.
  Past tense
<u>Will</u> you <u>jump</u> over the puddle?
  Future tense

Nouns name persons, places, or things.
List as many nouns as you can of things found on the Earth.
Names of cities, states, countries, etc., are "proper nouns." A proper noun always begins with a capital letter.
(Examples: America, God, Montana, France)

Science Scene

Materials Needed:
Pitcher, dry sand or fine, dry soil
Pictures of a sand dune, dust storm, and a glacier.
An ice cube, a penny, a nail.
Different types and colors of soil and rocks (or pictures of various types)
Magnifying glass, small scale to weigh rocks
Microscope, Computer and Internet, optional

Take a pitcher of water and pour it on the mountain of sand you formed during the Object Lesson. Begin close to the sand. Then raise the pitcher and pour it from a greater height to create more pressure.

What happens when the water runs down the sand mountain?
What happens when the water comes down with more force?
(You may continue this until most of the "mountain" is washed away.)

Water flowing down bare earth picks up soil and carries it downhill into a river or a lake. This is called erosion. Erosion can slowly wear away hillsides or river-banks.

Make a pile of dry sand or loose soil.
Blow on the soil. What happens? (Some of the soil is blown away.)
Wind also causes erosion.
Wind blows sand and loose soil.
The wind moves mountains of sand called sand dunes. (Show picture of a dune.)

Sometimes the wind blows so much soil that it creates a dust storm.
(Show picture of dust storm.)

Another type of erosion is caused by glaciers. (Show picture of a glacier.)
Take a large ice cube and rub it back and forth over the dry sand.
Turn the large ice cube over and show that some of the sand clings to the ice.
Glaciers carry along soil and rocks that rub on the earth as they slide across its surface. This wears away the earth below.

Sometimes a piece of a mountain or hill becomes unstable and falls down the side. This is called a landslide. Often this happens after lots of rain, like we saw when our sand mountain collapsed.

Our next lesson will show how God helps prevent erosion.

Show different types of soil (pictures or actual soil). Point to each one and name.
Sand, silt, and clay are the three basic types of soil.

If you have examples of soil:

- Feel the textures.
- Notice the colors.
- See how each type absorbs water.
- Look at the soil with a magnifying glass.
- Talk about how the soil types differ.

Science Scene, continued

SUMMARIZE:

Most soils are made up of a mixture of these three types: sand, silt, clay.

For Older Children:
Examine the soil where you live. Try to identify what kind it is.

Show various types of rocks. Talk about how they differ.
(Photo shows a fluorite rock)

The Earth's outer layer is made of three main types of rocks:

1. **Igneous rocks form when hot, melted rock (lava from volcanoes) cools, and hardens**. (Granite is one example.)

2. **Sedimentary rocks are formed from layers of sand, pebbles, and mud, such as happened after Noah's flood.**

The layers are squeezed together and turn into rocks over time. These rocks are softer and often chip or break easily. (Sandstone is one example.)

3. **Metamorphic rocks have been changed by great heat and pressure inside the Earth. These rocks are hard and strong.** (Marble is one example.)

(Photo of jasper rock)
Also: Look at rocks with a magnifying glass.

What do you notice about the different types? *(Below: Granite under a microscope)*

Weigh different rocks of similar size on a small scale.
Do rocks of the same size have the same weight? (No.)

Scratch different rocks to test their hardness. Use your fingernail, a penny, and a nail.
- **Soft rocks can be scratched by a fingernail.**
- **Medium hard rocks can be scratched by a copper penny.**
- **Harder rocks can be scratched by a nail.**
- **Very hard rocks, such as a diamond, can not be scratched by anything.**

For Older Children:
Look at various types of rock and sand under a microscope. Describe the difference.

Rocks come in many sizes, shapes, and varieties. Want to learn more? Check out the following website for more information:

www.masterbooks.org

Art Activity

Materials Needed:
Soil samples of different colors and texture such as garden soil, potting soil, clay soil, etc.
A variety of tiny rocks such as gravel, sand, lava rock, pebbles, small gemstones, shells, etc.
Clear jar
Melted wax, optional

Layer the soils and rocks in a clean jar to create a designer earth sculpture.

If you don't want it to shift or spill when tipped or shaken, melt wax to completely coat and seal the top of the soil sculpture inside the jar.

Set the jar out where it can enjoyed, especially during this week as you study LAND.

Extra Activity

Materials Needed:
Tumbled rocks or rock samples
Wooden or ceramic bowl

Find a local rock and gem store where your child can select some colorful stones to place in a box or a bowl. Set out on a table or counter and enjoy the variety of rocks and their many colors. Find rocks to add to your collection as you travel.

Visit this link for websites to view a variety of precious stones and their names including some magnificent specimens of the Smithsonian Gem & Mineral collection:

www.masterbooks.org

Spelling Spree

Materials Needed:
Paper and pencil
Heavy paper or cardstock
Scissors and marker

Choose words appropriate for the child's grade level/ability from this Creation lesson. (This can be done by the teacher or with the child.)
Examples: dunes, hill, sand, silt, clay, soil, rocks, igneous, sedimentary, metamorphic.

Have child read the list to you, pronouncing each word correctly and spelling it out loud. Make sure child knows the meaning of each word.

Teacher or child can write out the words on heavy paper or cardstock.

1. Cut the individual words into two to three pieces and mix up all the pieces.
2. Have child put the word puzzles together to form the spelling words.
3. The pieces may be glued onto a large piece of paper or saved to use again as a puzzle.

Give a spelling test at the end of the week.

Conclusion

tiger's eye rocks

Materials Needed:
Bible
The Creation Story for Children (optional)

The *Creation Story for Children* can be incorporated at this point by reading the account of Day Three up to the point where plants are created.

Ask questions about things you have studied in Lessons 1 through 4 as an oral quiz.

Read Proverbs 3:19–20. Talk about how great and wise God is in His role as Creator.

What is one of your favorite things in all of God's creation? Why?
What else are you glad God made?

Next time we'll learn about what grows on the land.

Thank God for the land, rocks, and soil, which are so important for us to be able to make our home here on earth.

Optional Discussion for Older Children:
Read Matthew 7:24–27, the Parable of the Wise Man who built his house on a rock.

What is the difference between building a house on the rock or on the sand?
What do we learn from this parable?

4

Lesson

Materials Needed:
Bible(s)
Heavy paper, marker

For Optional Activity:
Magazines, photos showing responsibility
Scissors, poster board, glue, markers
Computer with Internet, optional

Responsibility

God gave people the responsibility to care for the land He created.

What does it mean to be responsible? (Discuss.)

We should take good care of the things God has put in our charge.

If you have a garden, you pull the weeds so the plants have room to grow.

If you have a pet, you make sure it has the food and water it needs each day.

Doing your chores and taking good care of the things you own are ways of being responsible.

Character Connection

Being responsible and dependable pleases others and pleases God.

Does it show responsibility when Mom asks you to fold the clothes, and you wait until after you finish reading a book? (No.)

Does it show responsibility when Dad asks you to get his hammer, and you leave your game and hurry to obey? (Yes.)

Does it show responsibility when people pollute the land and water with garbage? (No.)

- **Responsible people do what they say they will. They don't let others down.**
- **Responsible people don't blame others or make excuses.**
- **Responsible people make good choices.**

Scripture Search
Proverbs 27:18   Ecclesiastes 9:10
Matthew 24:45–47   Luke 12:48b
Romans 14:12   Ephesians 6:5–8
Colossians 3:22–24

In what ways can you show you are a responsible person? (Encourage personal sharing. Talk about family chores.)

Responsible people always try to do their best. Is it "easy" to do your best?

Optional Activity:

Find pictures from magazines or photos from your own life of people acting responsibly. Create a collage by gluing these pictures onto poster board. You may add descriptions or write "Be Responsible" on it.

For Closing Discussion:

Why do you want to be thought of as responsible? (Encourage personal sharing.)

What are some of your personal responsibilities? (Homework, chores, etc.)

What are some rewards being a responsible person might bring? (Trust from others, privileges, feeling good about yourself, etc.)

How can you be responsible today? (Encourage personal sharing.)

RESPONSIBILITY Reminder:

1. Draw a large **R** on a heavy piece of paper.

2. Make a smiley face in the top of the **R** to remind you that being responsible makes everyone happy.

3. Place this **R** for responsibility on the fridge or hang it on your bedroom door.

- When you show responsibility, your **R** stands up straight and happy.

- When you fail to show responsibility, turn your **R** sideways so it faces down, sad.

- When you show responsibility, stand up your **R** straight and happy again.

Responsibility is reasonable and right.

Need more ideas for teaching or learning about the importance of responsibility? Find additional internet links at:

www.masterbooks.org

Materials Needed:

☐ **INTRODUCTION:**

Bible(s), different kinds of seeds

☐ **OBJECT LESSON:**

Large sheet of green construction
paper, scotch tape, scissors, small glass or jar,
Bible(s)

Different kinds of seeds in small
containers or sections of an egg carton

Flowers, plants, fruit, and vegetables

Or pictures of various plants that grow from the
seeds.

☐ **MATH CONNECTION**

Different shaped leaves — at least five
different types, pencil and paper

Computer and Internet, optional

☐ **ENGLISH/WORD WORK**

Paper and pencil

☐ **SCIENCE SCENE**

Wheat and flour, optional

Peanut butter and peanuts, optional

Jelly, jam, and fruit, optional

Picture of a plant with roots, stems, leaves, and
flowers, or a plant with all four parts

Computer and Internet, optional

Seeds to sprout and plant, optional

☐ **ART ACTIVITY**

Paper and crayon(s), unwrapped

Trees or tree bark, leaves, flowers

Catalogs, newspapers, and boards or other means
of pressing plants, optional

*"And God said, Let the earth bring forth grass, the herb yield-
ing seed, and the fruit tree yielding fruit after his kind, whose
seed is in itself upon the earth . . . and God saw that it was
good"* (Genesis 1:11–13 KJV).

Materials Needed, continued:

Cardstock, clear contact paper, wax paper, electric iron for
extra activities

☐ **SPELLING SPREE**

Paper and pencil

☐ **CONCLUSION:**

Bible , *The Creation Story for Children* book (optional)

Lesson Introduction

Materials Needed:
Bible(s)
Different kinds of seeds

Read Genesis 1:11–13.
Discuss any unfamiliar words.
Show a variety of seeds.
What grows from a seed? (A plant.)

**Can you tell what kind of plant will grow
by looking at a seed?** (No.)
But God knows.

onion bulbs

Object Lesson

Materials Needed:

Large sheet of green construction paper

Scotch tape and scissors, small glass or jar

Different kinds of seeds in small containers or sections of an egg carton

Flowers, plants, fruit, and vegetables *(or pictures of plants grown from the seeds)*

Paper and pencil and Bible(s)

- Roll up a large piece of green construction paper *(one-half of a sheet cut lengthwise).*
- Tape bottom of the roll to hold it together.
- With a scissors, make cuts through all the layers at the other end two to three inches long and about one-half inch apart around the roll.
- Hold this up with one hand on the uncut section. With the other hand, firmly grasp the inner edge of clipped end.

Watch this plant grow.

- Slowly pull the inner section up and allow the tube to stretch out, but remain in a roll.
- When fully extended, tape the sides to secure it, but leave the fringed section free.
- Have child help fold out the slits to make branches.
- Display your tree by placing its base in a small glass or jar to hold it upright.

The Bible tells us that all creation praises the Lord, even the trees. In Isaiah 55:12, it says that the mountains and the hills shall sing and the trees of the field will clap their hands. The trees will sing too.

Read Psalm 96:12.

- Set out containers or an egg carton with different kinds of seeds.
- Set out fruits, vegetables, flowers, and plants that grow from the seeds on display or use picture of these plants.
- Have child try to match the seeds with what they produce.
- Name the various fruit, vegetables, and plants you have on display.
- You might make a sign with its name to place beside each one.

When God created the first plants, He didn't start with seeds. He made full-grown plants appear on the Earth. These plants formed seeds to make new plants.

Read Ecclesiastes 2:5.

Talk about what grows in a garden and in an orchard. List all the different kinds of plants you can think of.

Grow beans, find worksheets, and more! Expand the scope of this lesson through web links available at:

www.masterbooks.org

Materials Needed:

Different shaped leaves—at least five different types

Paper and pencil

Computer and Internet, optional

1. Choose five different shapes of leaves. Draw the shapes and record your totals for each shape.
   Sort leaves by size:
   small to large, narrow to wide, etc.
   Record your answers.

2. Sort leaves by color. (If it isn't fall, use shades of green — light to dark.)
   Think of other ways to sort the leaves.
   Record your answers.

3. Count the points on each leaf-shape.
   Record your answers.

We are going to use leaves as pretend money today.

Assign a money value for each type of leaf: one cent, five cents, ten cents, twenty-five cents, and one dollar. (You may want to choose leaves containing more points as the ones with a larger value.)

Tape a small tag with the amount for that shape on one of each type of leaf to remind you what it's worth.

(Note: If you do not have lots of leaves of each shape for counting, trace the shapes and cut out copies of each shape.)

1. Beginning with the penny leaves, count the total amount of money.
   Record your total.

2. Continue counting each leaf value.
   Record the total of each kind.

3. ADD the totals to see how much you have all together.

4. Count all the leaf money to check your addition. Begin with the dollars.

How many quarters make one dollar?
(Four)

- ARRANGE your 25–cent leaves in piles of four to see how many dollars' worth you have.
  Record your answer.

- ADD this dollar amount to the total of your one-dollar leaves.
  Record your answer.

- SUBTRACT the sum of your ten-cent leaves from the total of the leaves worth 25 cents.
  Record your answer.

- Place the one–cent leaves in piles of ten.

- Place the five–cent leaves in piles of two.

Each of these piles is worth ten cents.

- COUNT by tens to find the total of cents and nickels.
  Record your answer.

MATH, continued

Which is the bigger amount — the sum of leaves in the piles that equal ten cents or the sum of the leaves worth ten cents each? (Count them if necessary.) How much more money is in the group that is worth more?

- ADD the sum of your ten-cent piles to the total of your ten-cent leaves. Record your answer.

Use your leaf money to make change and find equivalent amounts. Then make up your own money problems to solve.

If you could gather leaves for money, what would you buy?
God owns everything. Can we trust Him to give us all we need? (Yes!)

English Word Work

Materials Needed:
Paper and pencil

- **Adjectives describe nouns** (Persons, places, or things).

- **Adjectives help us picture things.**

- **Adjectives can tell how something looks, tastes, feels, or sounds.**

- **Adjectives answer questions like: How many? How big? What kind? Which?**

Find the adjectives in these sentences.
The tree is green.
Which word is the adjective? (Green)

"I dug up a long root."
Which word is the adjective? (Long)

"He found a pretty flower."
Which word is the adjective? (Pretty)

1. Write a noun (something created on Day Three) in the center of a large piece of paper.
2. Draw a circle around the noun.
3. Draw petals coming out from this circle.
4. Inside each petal write an adjective that describes the noun in the center.
5. Make a list of adjectives that tell about the things created on Day Three.
6. Use these adjectives in sentences or in a story.

For Older Children:
Create a journal or a newspaper about your neighborhood and what you observe. You could include the weather, the plants, gardening tips, a map, or whatever you like. You could also draw pictures or take photos to illustrate it.

Print and color a garden maze, and help a bee find its way through:

www.masterbooks.org

Materials Needed:
Wheat and flour, optional
Peanut butter and peanuts
Jelly, jam, and fruit, optional
Picture of a plant with roots,
stems, leaves, and flowers,
Computer and Internet, optional
Seeds to sprout and plant, optional

Think about all the foods you eat and how they are connected to plants. For example: Bread comes from flour that is ground from wheat — from the plant's seeds. (You may set out some wheat seeds and flour, or show a picture.)

Peanut butter comes from ground-up peanuts. These nuts grow under the ground from the plant's roots. (You may show peanut butter and peanuts.)

Jelly and jam are made from fruit, like grapes or strawberries. Fruit grows on plants to produce seeds. (You may show jam and the fruit from which it is made.)

Most plants have FOUR main parts: roots, stems, leaves, and flowers. Point to each of these parts on a plant or picture.

These parts may look different on different plants, but they each do a special job for the plant.
You can use vegetables to illustrate the parts of plants.

ROOTS:
- **Roots anchor the plant in the soil.**
- **Roots also help hold soil in place, which helps prevent erosion.**
- **Roots take food and water from the soil to feed the plant.**
- **Roots can store food for the plant. and sometimes roots are food for us, like carrots and potatoes.**

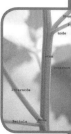

Look closely at some roots. Do you see the thin root hairs growing out from the main roots?

STEMS:
- **Stems carry the water and food up through the plant.**
- **Stems support the buds and leaves that grow on the plant.**

Explore different types of root illustrations and a website offering the use of vegetables to illustrate the parts of plants:

www.masterbooks.org

Science, continued

LEAVES:

- **Leaves take in air and give off oxygen into the air. Plants breathe through their leaves.**

- **Leaves take in sunlight to keep the plants healthy. The sun works through the leaves to make the plants green.**

FLOWERS & SEEDS:

- **Flowers & Seeds: Plants grow flowers to make seeds. Their seeds will grow new plants like the parent plants.**

LOOK AROUND YOU:
Next time you go grocery shopping, be on the lookout for plants.

Try to find some of each plant part: roots, stems, leaves and flowers.

Don't look only at fresh fruits and vegetables. Look in boxes (like corn flakes) and bottles (like tomatoes in catsup, bottles of fruit juice or vegetable juice) too.

Some medicines are also made from plants. Look in the herbal section of a health food store for dried herbs and bottles of herbs.

Visit this link for a website to view the life cycle of a bean plant or a website giving directions on how to sprout seeds inside a damp paper towel or a jar of water. For the older children, a website that teaches students about plant parts and photosynthesis or a site offering information on how to plan a garden:

www.masterbooks.org

Art Activity

Materials Needed:
Paper
Crayon(s), unwrapped
Trees bark
Leaves
Flowers

Optional: Catalogs, newspapers, and boards or other means of pressing plants
For Extra Activities: Cardstock, wax paper, clear contact paper, electric iron

1. Take plain sheets of paper and an unwrapped crayon outdoors.

2. Make rubbings of the bark of different trees by placing a piece of paper against the trunk and gently rubbing the side of the crayon back and forth to cover the paper.

3. Compare the different designs.

4. Try to draw a design that looks like the tree bark.

5. To make a leaf rubbing, place a leaf under a sheet of paper on a flat surface and rub the crayon gently over every part of the leaf.

6. Watch the leaf shape appear on your paper.

Extra Activity

Materials Needed:
Collect flowers and leaves.
Cardstock, clear contact paper, wax paper, electric iron

1. Place the flowers and leaves between pieces of white paper.
2. Put these in the middle of a heavy catalog or between newspapers with boards placed on top and weighted down to press the flowers and leaves.
3. Let them sit for several days until dry and flat.

You can glue the pressed flowers and leaves to cardstock to make pictures to frame. (Cover with glass to protect the pressed plants.)

You can place the flowers and leaves on clear contact paper and cover with another sheet of clear contact paper, or laminate them.

You can place the flowers and leaves between two pieces of wax paper and press with a warm iron. (NOTE: Only adults should use the iron.)

You can make greeting cards with your preserved flowers and leaves.

Spelling Spree

Materials Needed:
Paper and pencil

Choose words appropriate for the child's grade level/ability from this Creation lesson. **(This can be done by the teacher or with the child.)** Suggestions: flower, tree, leaf, leaves, stem, root, plant, grow, sprout, seeds, fruit, etc.

Have child read the list to you, pronouncing each word correctly and spelling it aloud.

Make sure child knows meaning of words. Write the list of words in alphabetical order.

Do any words begin with the same sound as your first name? List

Do any words begin with the same sound as your last name? List

Do any words begin with the same sound as your age? List

Which words have long vowels?

List and name the long vowels — a, e, i, o, u
When a word or syllable has a single vowel and the vowel appears at the end of the word or syllable, the vowel usually makes the long sound:

> no he go

Which words have short vowels?

List and name the long vowels — a, e, i, o, u
When there is a single vowel in a short word or syllable, the vowel usually makes a short sound. These short vowels usually appear at the beginning of the word or between two consonants.
Examples: c a t , e n d, p i g, l o g, b u s

Give a spelling test on the words at the end of the week.

Conclusion

Materials Needed:
Bible
The Creation Story for Children (optional)

Optional: Finish the account of Day Three in *The Creation Story for Children*, which shows how land was created and then plants.

Many plants are mentioned in the Bible. (Palm tree, fig tree, rose, lily, wheat, barley, spelt, etc.)

Which plants in our yard or house are your favorites? Why?

Which other plants would you like to have in our yard or house?

Keep a list of plants found in God's Word. Here are some places to look to get you started:

> Matthew 6:28, Genesis 8:11,
> Deuteronomy 23:24, Proverbs 25:11,
> Isaiah 17:19, Matthew 13:31–32.

Conclude your study with a prayer of thanks to God for the amazing array of plants in all of creation.

5

Lesson

Materials Needed:
Bible(s)
A crossword or Sudoku puzzle, tape
For Optional Activity:
Heavy kettle, large spoon, candy thermometer or a cup of cold water, greased pan, waxed paper, scissors, 2 cups white corn syrup, 1 tablespoon vinegar, 1 cup sugar, and 1 ½ teaspoons corn oil

Diligence

- A diligent person works hard.
- A diligent person doesn't give up when things get tough.
- A diligent person does his or her best.

God worked six days creating the universe.
After God created people, He told them to take care of His creation. This work included tending the plants God placed on Earth.
See Genesis 3:17–19, 23.

God told Adam and Eve they would have to work hard to grow food and to take care of the land.

Growing Vegetables Takes Diligence.
- **First, you must prepare the soil, getting rid of dirt clods and rocks.**
- **Then, you mark the rows where you want your crops to grow. You plant the seeds or little plants.**
- **Then you must keep the garden free of weeds and also water the plants.**
- **When the vegetables are ripe, you must harvest them.**
- **Then, you may have peas to shell or corn to husk.**
- **Maybe you help prepare food to can or freeze.**

Staying at a task takes diligence. How can you show diligence in your everyday life? (Encourage sharing.)

When you have a big assignment, like a report, how do you show diligence? (Keep working on the project until it is completed.)

Scripture Search

Deuteronomy 6:17	Joshua 22:5
Proverbs 6:5–8	Proverbs 10:4–5;
Romans 12:8, 11	1 Corinthians 4:2
Proverbs 13:4	1 Corinthians 15:58

What might happen if someone was not diligent? (Discuss.)

God blesses the efforts of the diligent.

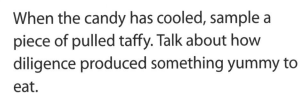

Optional Activity:

To demonstrate a reward of diligence, make a batch of pulled taffy.

You will need a heavy kettle, a large spoon, a candy thermometer or a cup of cold water, a greased pan, waxed paper, and a scissors.

Ingredients:
- 2 cups white corn syrup
- 1 cup sugar
- 1 tablespoon vinegar
- 1 ½ teaspoons corn oil

Combine these ingredients in a heavy kettle and stir. Bring to a boil and boil until it forms a ball when a spoonful is dropped into cold water (about 252° on a candy thermometer).

Pour this batter into a greased pan.

When the batter is cool enough to handle, take half or more of the batter and pull it until it's very soft. This works best with a partner. Each person takes an end and pulls, stretching the candy until it is long and thin.

Then fold it back into a small bunch and repeat the process until the taffy is soft and light-colored. The more you stretch it, the more tender it becomes.

Then, use a scissors to cut the long string of taffy into bite-size pieces onto the waxed paper. Individual pieces may be wrapped in waxed paper squares. Leave a portion of the candy batter in the greased pan.

When the candy has cooled, sample a piece of pulled taffy. Talk about how diligence produced something yummy to eat.

Now try to cut a piece from the portion that was left in the pan. Try to eat some of it.

Talk about how it is too hard to cut or chew.

The batter that was unworked turned hard. That part of the candy did not turn out like it should have. Why? (Discuss.)

Diligence produces good results.

For Closing Discussion:

- **How could not doing your work bring bad results?** (Discuss.)
- **Why is diligence important to help things go well?** (Discuss.)
- **What is one way you can be more diligent?** (Encourage personal sharing.)
- **How will you be diligent today?**

DILIGENCE Reminder:

Tape a hard crossword puzzle or a Sudoku puzzle by your mirror.

Just as it takes diligence to work a puzzle, we should put diligence to work in our daily life.

Do all with diligence.

God Creates Sun, Moon, Stars, & Planets

Materials Needed:

- [ ] **INTRODUCTION:** Bible(s)
- [ ] **OBJECT LESSON:**

Pencil and paper

Small birthday candle in a cup of dirt or something sturdy, a match

Computer and Internet, optional

- [ ] **MATH CONNECTION**

Pencil and paper, saucer or mechanical compass for drawing a circle, string or yarn, thumbtack, tape, ruler

An orange or other round fruit, knife

- [ ] **ENGLISH/WORD WORK**

Paper and pencil

- [ ] **SCIENCE SCENE**

Table lamp

Small ball, like a tennis ball, string

Computer and Internet, optional

Toilet paper, optional

- [ ] **ART ACTIVITY**

Card stock or heavy paper

Crayons of bright colors

Black crayon or tempera paint and paintbrush, nail or dry ink pen

- [ ] **SPELLING SPREE**

Paper and pencil, yellow crayon or marker, coins or game pieces

- [ ] **CONCLUSION:**

Bible, *The Creation Story for Children* book (optional)

> *"And God made two great lights . . . to rule over the day and over the night and to divide the light from the darkness: and God saw that it was good"* (Genesis 1:16–18 KJV).

Lesson Introduction

Materials Needed:
Bible(s)

Read Genesis 1:14–19.
Discuss any unfamiliar words.

What do we see in the sky at night?
(Moon and stars.)

What "star" do we see in the sky during the day? (The sun.)

The sun is just one small star among the millions of stars God created on Day Four.

Read: Psalm 8:1, 3; Psalm 104:19;
Psalm 147:4; and 1 Corinthians 15:41.

Object Lesson

Materials Needed:
Small birthday candle in a cup of dirt or something sturdy
Match
Computer and
Internet, optional

Place the birthday candle on a table. Turn off the lights so the room is dark. Then light the candle.

See how one small candle brightens the dark room.

Turn on the overhead light.
Does the candle seem very bright now?
(No.)

Turn the light off again to demonstrate that the candle's light has not changed.
This shows how a small light seems bright in the darkness.

When compared to brighter lights, the small light seems dim. Just like our sun seems very bright to us because it is near the Earth and so big compared to Earth, If we traveled to the bigger, brighter stars, the sun would seem to disappear.

The Bible says,
"[God] determines the number of the stars and calls them each by name"
(Psalm 147:4). (Have child repeat words of the verse after you.)

Photo of the Pleiades, a cluster of stars in the constellation of Taurus.

Compare the size of the Earth and other planets to the sun and to larger stars. There is also a link to a video showing the planets and stars from smallest to largest:

www.masterbooks.org

Math Connection

Materials Needed:

Pencil and paper
Saucer or mechanical compass for drawing a circle, String or yarn, thumbtack, tape, ruler, knife
An orange or other round fruit

- Trace a circle around a saucer or use a mechanical compass to draw a circle.

- You can also tie a short string to a pencil and tack the other end of the string in the middle of a piece of paper. Holding the pencil with the string stretched tightly, draw a circle around the center point.

- With a piece of string or yarn, measure the distance around the circle. (Tape one end to the circle and lay out the string around the circle until it reaches the place you began.)

- Mark or cut the string where it meets the other end.

- Lay this string in a straight line. (You may want to tape the ends to hold it tight.)

- With a ruler, measure the length of the string to find the distance around the circle. Record your answer.

If you could take the line that forms your circle and make it straight, this is how long it would be.

The distance around a circle is called its circumference. (That sounds sort of like "circle distance.")

- Use a ruler to draw a line across the middle of the circle to divide it in two. (You may want to fold your circle in half first to find the middle.)

The line that divides a circle into two equal halves is called the <u>diameter</u>. (The diameter divides.)

- Measure the length of the diameter of your circle with a ruler.
  Record your answer.
- Subtract the length of the diameter from the length of the circumference of your circle.
  Record your answer.

Is the difference of these two lengths more or is it less than the length of the diameter? (More.)

- Write Circumference > Diameter, with each word or symbol on a separate note card or piece of paper. (If necessary, explain greater than > and less than <.)
- Have child arrange these in the proper order to show which is greater.
- Reverse the > and arrange to show which is less.
  (Diameter < Circumference)

Math Connection, continued

How many strings as long as the diameter could you fit around the circle? (Three.)

- Demonstrate this with strings the length of the diameter, taping them around the circumference of the circle.

The circumference of a circle is more than three times as long as its diameter.

- Measure the circumference of an orange or any other round fruit. (Use a string and a ruler like you did for the circle.) Record your answers.
- Now cut the orange in half and measure the diameter across the cut section. Record your answer.
- Follow the steps used in comparing the diameter and circumference of the circle.

It doesn't matter whether a circle is flat or whether it is round like a ball, it has a circumference and a diameter.

The circumference of any circle is always greater than three times the length of its diameter.

- Find as many circles as you can today. Serve some round foods, like pizza, pancakes, etc.

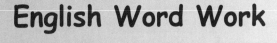

English Word Work

Materials Needed:
Paper and pencil

Words that rhyme end with the same sound, like day, play, say, weigh, hey.

Word endings do not have to be spelled the same, but must sound alike to rhyme.

Night and white rhyme, but use different letters to form the same sound.

List words that rhyme with each of these words:

> sun (fun, bun, run, pun, ton, won)
> big   (pig, rig, dig, fig, zig, wig)
> star   (car, far, jar, tar, bar)
> round (pound, ground, mound)
> bright (sight, fright, might, night)
> four (more, door, floor, pour, sore)

Can you find words that rhyme with your name?

Find rhyming adjectives and nouns that go together, like:

> funny bunny
> tall wall
> long song

Write sentences that end with rhyming words or create a poem.
(Look back at the weather poem in Lesson 2 for an example.)

61

Science Scene

Materials Needed:
Computer and Internet, optional
Table lamp, small ball (like a tennis ball)
String, toilet paper, optional

The EARTH:
The Earth we live on is like a big ball traveling through space.
The Earth is one of the planets that travel around the sun.

1. Place a lamp on a table.
   (If possible, remove the lampshade — avoid looking directly at the bright light.)

2. Attach a string to a tennis ball (or any small ball) or hold it from the top with just your thumb and forefinger.

3. Slowly move the ball in a circular orbit around the lamp.

4. EXPLAIN:
This is how the Earth goes around the sun. The Earth takes one year to go all the way around the sun.
The circular path the Earth travels around the sun is called an orbit.
Each planet has its own orbit or path around the sun.

5. LIGHT of the SUN:

Notice how the lamp lights only one side of the ball. In the same way, the sun lights only one side of the Earth at a time.

Where the sun shines on the Earth, it is day. What do we call the time where the Earth is in darkness? (Night.)

6. STARS:

There are millions of stars in the heavens. During the day, the bright light of the sun keeps us from being able to see the light of these faraway stars. When the sky is dark, we can see the stars shining in the sky.

Visit this link for a website offering comparisons of different planets, the sun, the moon, and the solar system:

www.masterbooks.org

Science Scene, continued

Go outside on a clear night, where there are not outside lights, and look at the stars and the moon. If you have access to a telescope, use it and be amazed at all the stars you can see. Find some constellations and the North star.

The MOON:

The moon orbits the Earth just like the Earth orbits the sun.

The moon reflects the light of the sun. It does not make its own light. As the moon moves around the Earth, we see different sides of the moon. These changes are called the moon's phases.

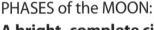

PHASES of the MOON:

A bright, complete circle is called a "full moon."

Then, the moon seems to get smaller until we see the dark side.

After that, we see the moon's light (the "new moon") and it grows larger until it becomes full again.

Observation Activity:

Observe the changes in the moon over the next month.

Every few days, draw pictures of how the moon looks.

Explore space with links to view a website viewing images from space (the Hubble Telescope), learn how to demonstrate how big our solar system is using a roll of toilet paper; discover more about astronomy with information and amazing photos; and see how the moon orbits the earth:

www.masterbooks.org

Art Activity

Materials Needed:
Card stock or heavy paper
Crayons of bright colors
Black crayon, or tempera paint
Paintbrush
Nail or dry ink pen

1. On card stock or heavy paper, color the entire page with bright colors in any design.
2. With a black crayon or black tempera paint, completely cover the colored page.
3. After it is dry, take a dried-out pen or a nail and scratch a picture on the black page. The colored design will show through.

This reminds us of God's bright stars shining throughout the blackness of space.

Spelling Spree

Materials Needed:
Paper and pencil
Yellow crayon or marker
Coins or game pieces

Choose words appropriate for the child's grade level/ability from this Creation lesson. (This can be done by the teacher or with the child.)

Examples: moon, sun, stars, night, day, darkness, light, planet, space, orbit, universe, diameter, circumference, etc.

Have child read the list to you, pronouncing each word correctly and spelling it aloud. Make sure child knows the meaning of each word.

Spelling Bingo:
- Make a grid on a sheet of paper, with five rows of five squares.

- Have child write one spelling word in each box, except in the center.

- Draw a yellow sun in the center box and write "free" across it.

Spelling Bingo, continued

If necessary, use spelling words from previous lessons to fill in the boxes.

Have child copy each word from the bingo grid onto separate pieces of paper.

Fold these each in half and mix in a bag. (If you have more than one student, choose more than 24 words so each card has some words the other doesn't on the bingo grid.)

Choose words from the bag one at a time and read each aloud.

Child marks the word on the bingo grid with a coin or game piece.

When a row of five is filled, across, up-and-down, or diagonally, child calls out, **"Bingo."**

Optional Ways to Play Spelling Bingo:
You might award a sticker for a "win" or trade places and let child choose and call out the words while you mark them on the grid.

You can also play until the bingo card is completely covered.

Give a spelling test on the words at the end of the week.

Conclusion

Materials Needed:
Bible
The Creation Story for Children (optional)

If you choose to incorporate *The Creation Story for Children*, read to the end of the account of Day Four. You can also do a quick review of the Creation days studied so far.

Read Psalm 148:1–6.

Verse 3 tells the sun, moon, and stars to praise the Lord. In what ways do the stars and other heavenly bodies praise God? (Think how they continue to rotate in their own cycles and pathways.)

In what ways can the planets and stars inspire us to trust God? (If God made such an awesome universe, then God certainly can take care of the details of our lives.)

Let's join these heavenly bodies in praising God for His marvelous creation — in the heavens above us and for our own planet Earth.

6 Lesson

Materials Needed:
Bible(s)
Penny, tape
For Optional Activity:
Paper, pencils, and small prizes like stickers, erasers, candy, gum, etc.

Trustworthiness

How do we know that the sun, moon, and stars are always in the sky, whether we can see them or not? (Because God placed them in space, and we know God is trustworthy.)

God created all things, and then said they were very good.

God set the laws of nature in order. We can trust that these laws will not change.

God made air for us to breathe. There won't be air to breathe one day and none the next. The moon won't stop its journey around the Earth. We can trust our Creator.

As God is trustworthy, so we should be people others can trust.

Character Connection

What do trustworthy people do?
Trustworthy people tell the truth.
Trustworthy people keep their promises.
Trustworthy people do what they say they will do.
Trustworthy people don't try to trick others.
Trustworthy people don't cheat.
Trustworthy people accept responsibility.

Scripture Search

Proverbs 20:7–11	Proverbs 11:3
Proverbs 23:23	Psalm 25: 5, 10, 21
Zechariah 8:16	Malachi 2:6
Romans 12:17	Ephesians 4:23–25

The Bible says that God hates lying (Proverbs 12:22).

What are some ways people are not honest? (Discuss.)

How could each example you gave change if the person was trustworthy?

We can make an acrostic from the word TRUST:

> **True**
> **Right**
> **Understanding**
> **Sincere**
> **Teachable**

A person who seeks to be True, Right, Understanding, Sincere, and Teachable will be trustworthy.

Optional Activity:

Play a game of THIEF with a group of children.

1. Gather small items, like stickers, erasers, gum, candy, etc. — have at least as many items as there are players, but not more than twice as many.
2. Lay these prizes out in the middle.
3. Pass out paper and pencil to each player.
4. Each player writes three numbers from one to ten on a piece of paper.
5. Call out the numbers, one at a time, in random order.
6. When players have a number you call, they grab a prize from the pile or they can "steal" a prize from another player.
7. When a prize is stolen, the person from whom it was taken may choose another prize, but cannot steal the same prize back on that turn.
8. Continue until all the numbers are called.

In a game, taking a prize seems fun, but how would you feel if someone really stole from you? (Encourage personal sharing.)

For Closing Discussion:
- **What would a trustworthy person do if he found someone's wallet full of money?** (Discuss.)
- **What would a trustworthy person do when someone tries to get her to do something her parents told her not to do?** (Discuss.)

- **Be careful what you say and do — this shows others whether or not they can trust you.**

- **Think about some ways you can show trustworthiness.**

Do you return things you borrow from others?
Do you make promises you will not be able to keep?
Do you finish the chores assigned to you?
Do you try to do what is right and good?
Do you treat others fairly? Do they trust you?

- **We need God's forgiveness when we fail to be trustworthy.**
- **We also need the forgiveness of others when we are not trustworthy.**
- **How will you be trustworthy today?**

TRUSTWORTHINESS Reminder:
Just like saving coins will add up to make dollars, so our deeds add up to create our character.

Carry a penny in your pocket or tape one on your clothes over your heart to remind you to be trustworthy.

Trust makes sense *(Sounds like cents.).*

God Creates Sea Creatures

Materials Needed:

☐ **INTRODUCTION:** Bible(s)

☐ **OBJECT LESSON:**
Quart jar or a large, clear glass
Small fish shape cut from foil (about two inches long), blue food coloring
Water, flashlight, pictures of sea creatures — especially those that live in the depths

☐ **MATH CONNECTION**
Pencil and paper, ruler, pictures of polygons with 3-12 sides, optional
Computer and Internet, optional

☐ **ENGLISH/WORD WORK**
Paper and pencil

☐ **SCIENCE SCENE**
Pictures of fish and other sea creatures
A whole fish to examine and cut open and a knife, optional
Computer and Internet, optional

☐ **ART ACTIVITY**
Heavy paper, such as cardstock or tagboard, glue, sand
Small seashells and/or shell designs and sea creatures cut from paper plates
Blue cellophane or blue paint
Computer and Internet, optional

☐ **SPELLING SPREE**
Paper, lemon juice, cotton swabs, toaster

☐ **CONCLUSION:**
Bible, *The Creation Story for Children* book (optional)

"God said, 'Let the waters bring forth abundantly the moving creature that hath life . . . and God created great whales and every living creature that moveth, which the waters brought forth abundantly, after their kind" (Genesis 1:20–21 KJV).

Lesson Introduction

Materials Needed:
Read Genesis 1:20–22.
Discuss any unfamiliar words.

Today we will be studying about the creatures God created to live in the water. These include fish of all types and sizes. One reason God created fish is for food for people.

Read Leviticus 11:9.

**Have you ever been fishing?
What did you use to catch fish?
Some people use fishing poles with hooks to catch fish.
Some fishermen use nets, like Jesus' disciples did.** (See Matthew 4:18 and Matthew 13:47–48.)

Lesson Introduction,
continued

What other creatures can you think of that live in the ocean?

You may ask questions to prompt ideas, such as:

> **What sea creature has eight legs?** (Octopus.)
> **What sea creature has a head that looks like a horse?** (Seahorse.)
> **What sea creature is clear and floats?** (Jellyfish.)

God made many kinds of sea creatures. The Bible tell us the creatures of the sea join in with the rest of creation in praising the Lord.

Wouldn't it be fun to see an octopus praise God? What do you think a whale would do to praise God? (Let children use their imaginations: whale slaps its tail or makes its special whale sound, etc.)

Read Isaiah 42:10.

Object Lesson

Materials Needed:
Quart jar or a large, clear glass
Small fish shape cut from foil (about two inches long)

Water, blue food coloring, flashlight
Pictures of sea creatures—especially those that live in the depths

- Before the lesson: Place the foil fish in the bottom of a jar. Fill the jar with water and add enough blue food coloring so that you cannot see through the water.

- Hold up the jar of blue water. **This dark-blue water reminds us of the oceans God created. Can you see anything in this water?** (No.)

- Shine the flashlight down into the jar from the top, then from the side. **Can you see anything now?** (If fish can be seen, ask, **"What do you see?"**)

- Shine the light up through the bottom of the jar. Look down from the top. **What do you see in the water?** (A fish). **God created many creatures to live in the sea. Some sea creatures live so deep in the ocean we never see them**.

- Show pictures of sea creatures.

Math Connection

Materials Needed:
Pencil and paper, ruler
Pictures of polygons with 3–12 sides, optional
Computer and Internet, optional

Today we will learn about polygons. Draw or show a picture of each shape.

When we studied Day Three of Creation, we talked about triangles.
How many sides does a triangle have?
(Three.)
How many sides does a square have?
(Four.)

A figure with five equal sides is called a pentagon (pen' tu gon").
A hexagon (hek' su gon") **has six equal sides.**

(Hexagon and six both have an X to help you remember how many sides.)

A heptagon (hep' tu gon") **has seven equal sides.**
An octagon (ok' tu gon") **has eight equal sides.**
What does an octagon make you think of?
(a stop sign)

A nonagon (non' u gon") **has nine equal sides.**
A decagon (dek' u gon") **has ten equal sides.**
A hendecagon (hen dek' u gon") **has eleven equal sides.**
A dodecagon (do dek' u gon") **has twelve equal sides.**

Repeat these names and the number of sides together several times.
Have child try to draw some of these shapes and label them.

Let's match some sea creatures with polygons.
What eight-legged sea creature would go with an octagon?
(an octopus)
Draw an octopus inside an octagon, with one leg going to each of the eight sides. Follow a similar procedure with the others.

Play math games with shapes, learn the names of any polygon up to one with 999 sides, and even how to count the sides of a polygon:

www.masterbooks.org

English Word Work

Materials Needed:
Paper and pencils

ROOT WORD:
A root word is the main part of a word. Other word parts may be added to the beginning or the end of a root word.

PREFIX:
**A word part that comes before the root word is called a prefix.
Prefix starts with the letter "P." A prefix peeks out before the main word.**

SUFFIX:
**A word part that comes after the root word is called a suffix.
Suffix begins with the letter "S." A suffix sneaks behind the main word.**

**Let's look at some root words and add prefixes and suffixes to them.
What new words can you form?**

Root Words	Prefixes	Suffixes
act	re-	-ed, -or,-tion, -tive
swim		-er
form	in-, re-	-al, -at, -ed, -er
fort	de-, im-, re-	-al, -er, -tion, -trait

**The root words might be a verb, but adding a suffix may change it to a noun. For example, the verb "act" + "tion" makes the noun "action."
Use some of these words in sentences.
Label them as nouns or verbs.**
(Make this activity appropriate to the child's reading level.)

Possible words:
 re + act = react
 act + ed = acted
 re + act + ed = reacted
 act + or = actress
 act + tion = action
 act + tive = active
 swim + er = swimmer
 in + form = inform
 form + al = formal
 in + form + al = informal
 form + ed = formed
 in + form + ed = informed
 re + form = reform
 re + form + ed = reformed
 form + at = format
 re + form + at = reformat
 form + at + ed = formatted
 form + er = former
 re + form + er = reformer
de + port = deport (-ed can also be added)
im + port = import (-ed can also be added)
re + port = report (-ed can also be added)
 port + al = portal
 port + er = porter
 port + tion = portion
 port + trait = portrait

Science Scene

Materials Needed:
Pictures of fish and other sea creatures
A whole fish to examine and cut open and a knife, optional
Computer and Internet, optional

God made many different kinds of creatures to live in the ocean.
One of the most common animals that live in water is a fish. There are many, many different kinds of fish.

Show pictures of fish and other sea creatures as you ask: **What are some of your favorite sea creatures?**

If you have a fish, observe its eyes, mouth, teeth, gills, scales, fins, backbone, etc., as you mention them.

EYES:

A fish has one eye on each side of its head.

MOUTHS:

Fish can live underwater because they do not breathe air.
Fish take in water through their mouths. That is why you see fish open their mouths so often.

GILLS:

Fish get oxygen from the water that comes in through their mouths. Then fish send the rest of the water out through their gills. Can you find the slits on the sides of the fish's head? Those openings are the "gills."

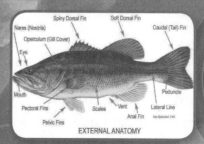

EXTERNAL ANATOMY

SCALES:

Can you see what is all over the fish's body? Most fish have scales covering their skin.

FINS:

What do you think helps a fish move through the water? (Fins.)
Most fish have fins to help them swim. How many fins does this fish have?

COLD–BLOODED:

Fish and other sea creatures are called cold–blooded animals. They are called cold–blooded because they take on the temperature of their surroundings. They are hot when their environment (the ocean water) **is hot and cold when their environment is cold**

BACKBONES:

Fish have backbones with small bones coming out from the long backbone. If you have a fish to examine, filet it and observe the bones.

Science Scene, continued

Some sea creatures, like an octopus, sea slugs, starfish, crabs, sponges, snails, or jellyfish, do not have a skeleton or a backbone.

Do you think a whale or a dolphin or a shark has a backbone? (Yes)

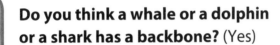

Visit this link for websites to Learn about fish and other animals of the sea like sharks, whales, octopi, seashells, and a website with an imaginary submarine to view sea creatures:

www.masterbooks.org

Art Activity

Materials Needed:
Heavy paper, such as cardstock or tag-board
Glue
Sand
Small seashells
and/or shell designs
and sea creatures cut
from paper plates
Blue cellophane or blue paint
Computer and Internet, optional

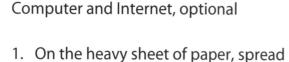

1. On the heavy sheet of paper, spread glue solidly across the bottom about three inches wide.

2. Sprinkle sand over the glue to cover it.

3. Arrange seashells and sea creature figures on the sand.

4. Glue them in place.

5. Allow to dry.

Extra Activity

- If using cellophane, you may glue sea shells and sea creatures anywhere on the paper.

- Glue the cellophane all around the edges of the paper. You may leave it crinkly so it looks like waves.

- If using blue paint, paint the portion above the dry sandy area.

- When the paint is dry, glue on the sea shells and sea creature figures so some are in the water.

Get directions for how to make an octopus wind dancer, a website giving directions how to make a cardboard shark, or a cardboard shark, or other ocean creature craft ideas:

www.masterbooks.org

Spelling Spree

Materials Needed:
Paper
Lemon juice
Cotton swabs
Toaster

crab

Choose words appropriate for the child's grade level/ability from this Creation lesson. (This can be done by the teacher or with the child.)
Examples: sea, ocean, creatures, fish, crab, fins, gills, scales, octopus, shark, triangle, square, root word, prefix, suffix, etc.

Have child read the list to you, pronouncing each word correctly and spelling it aloud. Make sure child knows the meaning of each word.

Spelling Activity:
Have child write the spelling words with invisible ink using lemon juice and cotton swabs.

After the page is dry, hold the paper over a warm toaster until the words appear. Be careful not to touch the paper to the toaster so it won't catch fire.

Check to see the words are spelled correctly.

Give a spelling test on the words at the end of the week.

Conclusion

Materials Needed:
Bible
The Creation Story for Children (optional)

The Creation Story for Children can be incorporated at this point by reading the first half of the account of Day Five.

1. **In Job 28:18, we read of coral from the sea** (see photo).

This verse says that wisdom is worth much more than earthly treasures.

- **Think about your need for wisdom. Why do you need wisdom? Ask God to give you wisdom for the choices you make in your life today.**

2. **Knowing the all–wise God of creation is much more wonderful than just knowing about His creation.**

- **Take time today to tell God how much you enjoy His vast creation.**

- **Then take time alone outside to sit and enjoy God. Think about how much this almighty Creator–God loves and cares for you and me.**

Lesson 7

Character Connection

Working together with someone else makes the work easier and faster. It's also more fun to work with another person than to work alone.

Cooperation means working together and helping each other.

Cooperation means taking turns and sharing.

Cooperation means solving problems together.

Can you cooperate if you don't listen to others? (No.)

What might happen when someone doesn't listen to instructions? (Discuss.)

Scripture Search

Proverbs 15:22	Ephesians 5:21
1 Corinthians 10:33	Galatians 6:2
2 Corinthians 6:1	Philippians 2:1–4
1 Thessalonians 3:12	

Plan ways to work together at home to make things go more smoothly. Cooperation doesn't just happen — it takes effort to succeed.

When people cooperate, it is better for everyone. (Remember how cooperation while pulling taffy made the candy turn out well?)

Materials Needed:
Bible(s)
String

For Optional Activity:
A big pile of clean family laundry

Cooperation

Some of the sea creatures God created cooperate to help each other out.

- **The little cleaner shrimp uses its claws to pick stuff from fishes' bodies and even get inside their mouths to clean their teeth.**

- **The shrimp helps the fish keep clean and uses what it finds on the fish for food. These sea creatures cooperate for the good of both.**

Co means "with" or "together."

Operate means "to act" or "to work."

Co + operate = Cooperate. Together this makes the word cooperate.

Optional Activity

- As you do the family laundry, fold laundry into piles on your bed.

- Instruct child to fold all items into separate piles.

- After child works a while alone on this overwhelming task, join him and help fold and sort.

- Have other family members take part too.

- Observe how much easier and quicker it is to work together and get the job done. Each person recognizes his or her own clothes, so you don't need to wonder what is whose. (You might sing "When We All Work Together.")

For Closing Discussion:
How can cooperation make others feel needed?

What are some ways your family cooperates? (Encourage personal sharing.)

We should also cooperate with God in the work He wants to accomplish.

Look for ways to cooperate each day. What is something you can do today to cooperate?

COOPERATION Reminder:

Sometimes people tie a piece of string around their finger to remind them of something special.

Have someone tie a string around your finger or your wrist — this takes cooperation as you both work together.

Whenever you see this string, remember that cooperation is good for everyone.

Cooperation means good relations. Let's encourage each other each day to cooperate.

Lesson 8

God Creates Birds

Materials Needed:

- ☐ **INTRODUCTION:** Bible(s)
- ☐ **OBJECT LESSON:**

Bag to hold objects for Object Lesson

Styrofoam egg

Beak cut from yellow plastic (lid)

Two large-headed straight pins

Brown or yellow chenille wire, bent into two bird legs 3" long (three–toed feet)

Two feathers, or stiff paper cut into wing shapes, and two straight pins

Small feathers and glue, optional

- ☐ **MATH CONNECTION**

Pencil and paper

Computer and Internet, optional

- ☐ **ENGLISH/WORD WORK**

Paper and pencil

Computer and Internet, optional

- ☐ **SCIENCE SCENE**

Pictures of different birds

Encyclopedia or bird book, optional

Computer and Internet, optional

- ☐ **ART ACTIVITY**

Milk or juice ½–gallon carton

Ruler, sharp knife (screwdriver, optional)

Four ¼-inch dowels about 3.5 inches long Wild bird seed, duct tape

Wire coat hanger or a piece of wire

Computer and Internet, optional

- ☐ **SPELLING SPREE**

Paper and pencil

- ☐ **CONCLUSION:**

Bible, *The Creation Story for Children* book (optional)

"God created . . . every winged fowl after his kind: and God saw that it was good. And God blessed them, saying, Be fruitful, and . . . let fowl multiply in the earth" (Genesis 1:20–21 KJV).

Lesson Introduction

Materials Needed:

Bible(s)

Read Genesis 1:20–23.
Discuss any unfamiliar words.

Today we will study more about the fifth day of Creation.
First, let's review what we learned in the first seven lessons.

On Day One, God created _____ (light)
On Day Two, God created the __ (sky)
On Day Three, God created the_____ ,
_____, and _____ (water, land, plants).
On Day Four, God created the _____,
_____, and _____(sun, moon, stars).
Last time we learned that God created
____ _____ on Day Five (sea creatures).

Object Lesson

Materials Needed:
(Note: Place these materials in a bag so they can't be seen until you pull each out.)

Styrofoam egg
Beak cut from yellow plastic (lid)
Two large–headed straight pins
Brown or yellow chenille wire, bent into two bird legs 3" long, with three–toed feet
Two feathers, or stiff paper, cut into wing shapes, and straight pins to hold them
Small feathers and glue, optional

Before showing what's in the bag, say:
We are going to learn about something that has two eyes, (Point to the body parts as you name them.) **Two ears, two nostrils, two legs, two feet, and two wings**.
(Move arms in a
wing–like motion.)

- Show the Styrofoam egg.
  This creature comes from an egg.

- Hold the egg near your ear.
  I think I hear something peeping. The egg must be ready to hatch.

- Poke the yellow plastic beak into the small, pointed end of the egg, so the beak looks slightly open.
  Something is trying to get out of its little egg home.

- Poke in the large–headed pins for eyes, one on each side above the beak.

- Stick the chenille legs into the bottom of the egg so the chick will stand up.

- Poke one wing into each side of the bird about halfway down.

  (If you use paper wings, secure them with straight pins.)

- Stand the bird on a table.

Our little bird has hatched. All birds come from eggs.

- If you have small feathers, rub glue on the Styrofoam, then cover the chick with feathers to make it look more like a bird.

After a chick hatches, its wet feathers need to dry out. Then the baby chick is soft and fluffy.

- Let the chick set to dry if glue is used.

Today we are going to learn more about birds. God created birds on Day Five.

Assortment of eggs from birds and reptiles:

Math Connection

Materials Needed:
Pencil and paper
Computer and Internet, optional
Note cards, optional

We just talked about the "twos" on a bird. Let's count how many twos we can find.

Write these twos on a piece of paper:

Two eyes
Two ears
Two feet
Two legs
Two knees
Two wings
Two nostrils

Can you think of any more parts a bird has two of? (Add to the list if you can.)

We call two of the same thing a pair, like a pair of shoes or a pair of gloves. Let's add the total of twos we found on a bird.

Add the twos as you
go down the line, like this:

2 + 2 = 4.
4 + 2 = 6.
6 + 2 = 8.

Keep adding until you reach the end of your list.
You might practice writing problems as equations, as shown above, and also in columns to solve, like this: 12
+2
14

Now let's count these groups of two by twos.
Point to each group on the list as you count.
Two, four, six, eight, ten, . . . (to the end of your list)
Did we get the same final total both times? (Yes.)

How many groups of twos do we have?
(Allow child to count if needed. If you have more that seven groups listed, use that number.)
Write the total number of groups: 7
Write the number in each group: x 2
Add the times sign and multiply: 14

We have found three ways to find the same answer.

   1. **We can add the numbers.**
   2. **We can count by twos.**
   3. **We can multiply.**

Make sure child understands each method.

Math Connection, continued

If you are just introducing multiplication, practice multiplying by two:

2 x 1 =   2 x 2 =
2 x 3 =   2 x 4 = etc.

Extra Activity:
The child could use note cards to make flash cards, with the problem on one side and the answer on the other side.
This will reinforce the math facts.

English Word Work

Materials Needed:
Paper and pencil
Note cards, optional
Computer and Internet, optional

Words that have the same meaning are called synonyms.
Close and near are synonyms.
Autumn and fall are synonyms.

What is a synonym for glad? (Happy.)
What is a synonym for penny? (Cent, coin)

Words can have more than one synonym. Unhappy, sad, and gloomy are all synonyms.
Have child list as many synonyms as possible, then pick one or more of these to do:

- Choose some synonyms to illustrate.

- Use some synonyms in a story.

- Make a matching game using synonym pairs.

- Write each word on a separate card.

Visit this link for websites to practice multiplication by 2, a printable fill-in counting book about penguins, and websites to help you practice finding and using synonyms:

www.masterbooks.org

Science Scene

Materials Needed:
Pictures of different birds (named below)
Encyclopedia or bird book, optional
Computer and Internet, optional

There are over 8,500 different kinds of birds.
Show pictures of various birds as you talk about them.

Birds are warm–blooded animals, with two legs and two wings. Birds' bodies are covered with feathers. Birds have beaks, but no teeth.

Most birds can fly. They have hollow bones and strong flight muscles. Birds that fly have wings that are shaped to help them fly. The feathers of a male bird are usually more colorful than a female bird's.

FOOD:
Different birds eat different things. Many birds eat insects. Some, like swallows, catch their meal in flight. Some birds, like chickadees, eat seeds. They love birdfeeders. Some birds, like eagles and hawks, eat meat. You have probably seen a robin catching a worm in the grass. Other birds, like toucans, eat fruit. Birds that drink nectar from plants, like hummingbirds, also help pollinate flowering plants (just like bees do).

NESTS:
Birds make nests. The mother bird lays eggs in the nest. Most birds sit on their eggs to keep them warm so they will hatch.
Some birds, like chickens, lay an egg every day. Other birds lay one batch of eggs in the spring. When the baby birds hatch, the parents keep busy bringing the baby birds food.

SONGS:
Most birds sing. Each type of bird has its own special sound.

PENGUINS:
Penguins can't fly. Penguins' small wings act like flippers and help them swim.

OSTRICH:
The ostrich is the largest bird. It grows up to nine feet tall. Ostriches can't fly either, but they can run very fast.

BEE HUMMINGBIRD:
The smallest bird is the bee hummingbird. It is only two-and-one-half inches long. (Show the length with your fingers or use a ruler.)

Science Scene,
continued

Hummingbirds are
the only birds that
can fly backwards
and move up and
down like a
helicopter.

BIRDS IN THE BIBLE:
**Many birds are mentioned in the Bible.
How many different birds can you find in
these passages?**

List the birds.
You might look each one up in an encyclopedia or bird book or
online.

[Note: The birds from
the Holy Bible, King
James Version, are
listed.]

Leviticus 11:13–19
(The names of birds vary in different Bible
versions — you can compare lists.)
Nineteen birds are mentioned: eagle,
ossifrage, ospray, vulture, kite, raven,
owl, night hawk, cuckow, hawk, little owl,
cormorant, great owl, swan, pelican,
gier eagle, stork, heron, and lapwing.
    (NOTE: The bat is not a bird.)

Isaiah 35:11 (cormorant, bittern, owl, raven)
Psalm 55:6 (dove)
Isaiah 40:31 (eagle)
Job 39:26 (hawk)
Job 39:13 (peacock, ostrich)
Genesis 15:9 (pigeon, turtledove)
Psalm 105:40 (quail)
Job 38:41 (raven)
Psalm 84:3 (sparrow, swallow)
Jeremiah 8:7 (stork, turtle[dove],
swallow, and crane)
Luke 2:24 (turtledove, pigeon)

**Have more fun learning about birds
(hummingbirds, penguins, eagles, etc.),
as well as information on state and national birds:**

www.masterbooks.org

Materials Needed:
Milk or juice ½–gallon carton
Ruler, sharp knife, wild bird seed, duct tape Screwdriver, optional
Four ¼–inch dowels about 3.5 inches long
Wire coat hanger or a piece of wire
Computer and Internet, optional

- Open the entire top of the empty carton.
- Wash the carton with warm, sudsy water and rinse well. Dry the inside.
- Measure one inch up from the bottom of the carton at each corner. Mark lines one-inch long out from the edges on each side.
  (Note: See picture of carton from Oregon Dept. of Fish and Wildlife.)
- Have an adult use a sharp knife to cut along the lines at each bottom corner.
- About two inches above the slits, push in on the outside edges and indent them (as shown). This will make a square opening at each bottom corner.

- On opposite sides of the carton, use the point of the knife or a screw driver to poke a small hole in the carton about one-half-inch up from each bottom corner.

- Insert a dowel into each hole for a bird perch.
- Fill the bird feeder with wild birdseed.
- Close the top of the carton and fasten it with duct tape (to keep the rain out).

- Attach a wire coat hanger or a piece of wire to the middle of the top of the carton so you can hang up the bird feeder.
- Hang it from a tree or a hook from the house eaves.

Note: Be sure to keep the feeder filled because the birds will depend on it and will continue to come eat daily. Enjoy watching feathered friends come visit.

(It may take several days or up to two weeks for birds to find the feeder.)

Discover how to make a bird mobile with a nest and eggs, or one with paper cranes. You can even learn how to create a pretend bird's nest with eggs. For younger children, print out some of the coloring pages featuring birds:

www.masterbooks.org

Spelling Spree

Materials Needed:
Paper and pencil

- Choose words appropriate for the child's grade level/ability from this Creation lesson. (This can be done by the teacher or with the child.) Examples: bird, nest, song, wings, beak, feathers, synonym, etc.

- Have child read the list to you, pronouncing each word correctly and spelling it aloud. Make sure child knows the meaning of each word.

- Create a riddle about each spelling word, with the answer being the word.

- When a riddle is asked, child must spell and state the word.

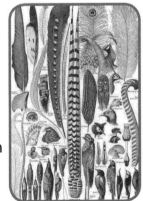

Give a spelling test on the words at the end of the week.

Conclusion

Materials Needed:
Bible
The Creation Story for Children (optional)

Optional: Finish the account of Day Five in *The Creation Story for Children*, which shows how creatures of the sea and then the air were created.

Birds are important to God. God takes good care of all the birds. Birds were the first animals to leave the Ark after the flood.
(See Genesis 8:7–12.)

Read Matthew 6:26. (Include 27–34 for older children.)

How can a little bird remind you of God's care? (Helps us remember God can feed us too, so why worry?)

How can a flower remind you of God's care? (Helps us remember God can provide our clothing and all we need.)

As God cares for the birds and feeds them, God also takes care of us. Let's thank God for His creation of thousands of birds.

Insect catching

Coniferous-seed eating

Fruit eating

Dip netting

Mud probing

Filter feeding

Pursuit fishing

Raptorial

Grain eating

Nectar feeding

8

Lesson

Materials Needed:
Bible(s)
Bird cutout or paper crane
Thread for hanging

For Optional Activity:
Computer with Internet, optional
Origami paper or paper squares for folding

Peaceableness

Imagine a beautiful flower garden with birds singing on a sunny spring day. This scene sounds peaceful. It should be a place where you feel happy and relaxed.

But sometimes a peaceful place does not bring peace to a person who feels upset and unhappy.

Peace can't just be "on the outside." Where does real peace need to be? (Real peace needs to be on the inside. We need to have peace in our hearts.)

Where can we find true peace? True peace comes from God. The outside world may be peaceful or wild, but we can still have peace inside.

Character Connection

- **What does a peaceful person do?**
A peaceful person spreads peace to others.
Peaceable people are just and fair.
Peaceable people don't fight or demand their own way.
Peaceable people try to make peace with others when they don't get along.
Peaceable people look for ways to make life smoother.

We want to have peace in our family and in our home.
We want to have peace in our neighborhood and in our town.
We want peace in our nation and peace in the whole world.

- **We should pray for God's peace. Let's ask God to help us be peacemakers.**

> **Peace**

- **What did Jesus say about peacemakers? He said, "Blessed are the peacemakers …"** (Matthew 5:9).

Scripture Search

Leviticus 19:15	Proverbs 4:18
Isaiah 26:3	Romans 12:10, 18
Philippians 2:14	1 Timothy 5:21
James 2:1, 8	James 3:17-18
1 Peter 3:11	

- **Whenever you start to feel mad, what can you do?**

Stop and think about the problem.

Anger always makes things worse.

How can you help make things better?
(discuss)
1. **Can you talk about the problem and find a solution?**
2. **Pray! Ask God to help bring peace.**

Jesus promised (in John 14:27) **to give His followers peace.**

> **Pausing to pray for peace is always a good plan.**

Optional Activity

At the website http://www.sadako.org/ you can find a story about a Japanese girl and her efforts to promote peace.

Click on the "Sadako project" link at the left, then scroll to the bottom and click on "Sadako story."

There are also a song and a poem, plus directions for folding a paper crane. A link to animated directions is on the home page.

Practice folding paper cranes. You might give them to others to encourage living in peace.

For Closing Discussion:

How can you practice peace — with brothers and sisters and with friends? (Discuss.)
When is it the most difficult to get along with others? (When they get angry, or when they cheat or lie or talk about you behind your back.)

How can you practice peace while playing a game? (Discuss.)

Would you rather play with a poor loser or a good sport? Why?

Peaceable people are good sports, whether they win or lose.
When have you been a good sport?
How will you be peaceable today?

PEACEABLENESS Reminder:
Birds are often associated with peace, like the dove of peace.
- Hang a paper crane or a bird-shaped cutout from a ceiling light.
- Every time you see this bird think about how you can work for peace.

Whether you work or whether you play,
do everything
in the most peaceable way.

Lesson 9

Materials Needed:

☐ **INTRODUCTION:** Bible(s)
☐ **OBJECT LESSON:**
Rocks piled up to form a cave
Soil in a container with a burrow dug out.
A tree branch or a small tree stuck in a container.
Pictures of animals and their homes
Computer and Internet, optional

☐ **MATH CONNECTION**
Pencil and paper, also graph paper
Colored pencils or crayons, mirror
Pictures of symmetrical shapes or objects
(a butterfly, snowflake, raindrop, ball, etc.)
A picture of an animal face–front or a
stuffed animal
Picture from magazine

☐ **ENGLISH/WORD WORK**
Paper and pencil
Computer and Internet, optional

☐ **SCIENCE SCENE**
Computer and Internet, optional

☐ **ART ACTIVITY**
Paper and tempera paint

☐ **SPELLING SPREE**
Graph paper, paper, and pencil
Scissors

☐ **CONCLUSION:**
Bible, *The Creation Story for Children* book (optional)

"And God said, Let the earth bring forth the living creature after his kind, cattle, and creeping thing, and beast of the earth after his kind: and it was so . . . and God saw that it was good" (Genesis 1:24–25 KJV).

Lesson Introduction

Materials Needed:
Bible(s)

Read Genesis 1:24–25 together.
Discuss any unfamiliar words.

**Today we will learn about creatures God made on the sixth day of Creation.
God had already made creatures to live and swim in the water.**

God had already made birds to fly and nest on the land.

Now, God was ready to create insects and four-legged creatures to fill the Earth.

God made all the many different wild animals.

Lesson Intro, continued

God made all the animals people use on farms and have for pets.

What animals are good pets? What pets do you or your friends have?

What day of Creation were these kinds of animals (your pets) first made? (Day Six for animals, Day Five for birds and fish)

Object Lesson

Materials Needed:
Rocks piled up to form a cave
Soil in a container with a burrow dug out
A tree branch or small tree stuck in a container
Pictures of animals and their homes
Computer and Internet, optional

Show pictures of the animal and their homes as you talk about them. (Examples of animals are given for each habitat.)

Point to the rock cave.
What kinds of animals live in a rock cave? (Bear, tiger, lion, wolf, bat,

Point to the burrow.
What kinds of animals live in a hole in the ground? (Rabbit, fox, mouse, mole, gopher, skunk, ferret, weasel, armadillo, prairie dog, ant, worm, snake, etc.)

Point to the tree.
What kinds of animals live in a tree? Squirrel, raccoon, monkey, chimpanzee, etc.

Point to a barn.
What kinds of animals live in a barn? (Horse, cow, sheep, goat, pig, mouse, etc.) **God created many different animals, with different habits and homes.**

Underground Ant home:

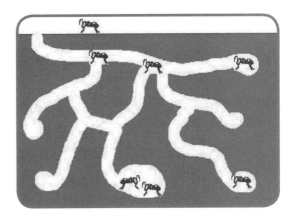

Visit this link for websites to see examples of animal homes:

www.masterbooks.org

Math Connection

***Materials Needed:*:**
Pencil and paper
Graph paper
Pictures of symmetrical shapes or objects
(like a butterfly, snowflake, raindrop, ball)
A picture of an animal face–front or a
stuffed animal
Computer and Internet, optional
Mirror and picture from magazine
Colored pencils or crayons

SYMMETRY:
**Some objects or
designs can be divided
in the middle so that
both sides match exactly.
This is called symmetry.**

Show symmetrical shapes, such as a ball,
a butterfly, a snowflake, a raindrop.

DISCUSS SYMMETRY:
**What are some things
that have symmetry?**

Look at flowers, like a daisy,
find faces of animals, etc,
Keep a list of all you find,
including letters of the alphabet.

**When you look at an animal from the
front or the back, its body
shape has symmetry.**

Demonstrate with a picture
or hold up a stuffed animal.

- **Each side of the face has an eye.**
- **Each side of the face has an ear.**
- **A line down the middle divides the
  nose and the mouth in half.**
- **Each side is like a mirror image of
  the other**.

ACTIVITY TO SHOW SYMMETRY:
1. Take a picture from a magazine and
   fold back one half or cut it in half.

2. Hold the half-picture up to a mirror to
   make a complete picture in symmetry.

Optional Activity:
1. Divide a sheet of graph paper in half
   (vertically or horizontally).

2. Create a design that is the same on
   both halves. (Colored pencils can be
   erased if an error is made.)

3. To check your creation for symmetry,
   fold it in half and see if both sides
   match.

English Word Work

Black–and–white animals:

Materials Needed: Paper and pencil, crayons, computer and Internet, optional

In Lesson Eight we learned about synonyms. What are synonyms?
(Words that have the same meaning.)

Today we will learn about words that have opposite meanings. Two words that mean the opposite are called antonyms, like dark and light, thick and thin, up and down, hot and cold, fast and slow, black and white, etc.

Have child list as many antonyms as possible.
Look at your list of synonyms. Find antonyms for as many as you can.

Create an illustrated antonym dictionary, with pictures to show the meanings of the words.

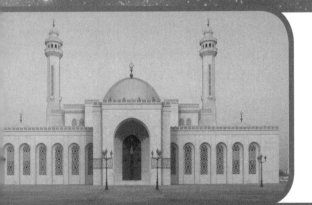

Get more lessons, videos, and a fun quiz about symmetry, and websites with amtonym matching games:

www.masterbooks.org

Science Scene 1

Materials Needed for #1:
Pictures of various animals

God Creates Animals

God created living creatures on the land on Day Six. These living creatures include all kinds of animals, wild and tame; insects and creeping things.

A Huge Animal

The largest land animal alive today is the African bush elephant. A baby elephant calf may weigh 225 pounds at birth, more than most grown men. The biggest adult elephant weighed 27,000 pounds. (How many tons is that? 2,000 pounds equal one ton, so that would be 13½ tons.)

This big elephant stood over 13½ feet tall at his shoulder. From the tip of his trunk to the end of his tail, he measured 35 feet. (You might measure that distance to "see" how long he was.)

God not only made large creatures, like an elephant, hippopotamus, and rhinoceros, He created tiny life life forms too (like crickets and ants).

A Tiny Animal — Jaragua Lizard

The littlest lizard alive is less than 1½ inches long. This dark-brown lizard is said to be the smallest of all 23,000 kinds of reptiles, birds, and mammals known to scientists.

The teeny lizard is just one of several very small creatures found in the Caribbean. This island area is also home to the smallest frog in North America and the world's smallest bird and snake. (See threadsnake on a quarter.)

Camels

God made desert animals, like dromedaries (with one-hump) **and camels** (with two humps)**. Camels can go without water for days in the heat. Then a camel may drink 26 to 40 gallons of water in one drink!** (That's enough water to fill a bathtub.)

Jungle and Forest Animals

God made jungle animals to live among the thick trees, like monkeys that swing by their tails, and also chimpanzees and gorillas.

Science Scene 1, continued

Big "cats" also live in the jungles. The leopard's spots help them hide in the shadows. What other animals live in the jungle? (Tigers, jaguars, sloth, tapir.)

God also made animals like bear, elk, deer, and squirrels to live in the forest. How many forest animals can you name? Which ones have you seen?

Water Animals

God made river animals and animals that live in lands of snow and ice. Where do beavers and otters live?
(By a river or pond.)
What large white animal lives in the frozen North? (Polar bear.)

Farm Animals

What animals might you find on a farm? (Cow, horse, pig, donkey, mule, goat, sheep) How do these tame animals help people? (Pull heavy loads, provide food and wool, etc.)

Other Creatures

God also made snakes and spiders and bugs, things we sometimes consider creepy and crawly. But many of these creatures help our environment. Friendly earthworms help work the soil. They live underground.

Dangerous rattlesnakes have poisonous venom. They often live in rocky areas and like to lie in the warm sunshine. Watch out!

Spiders help people and farmers when they eat flies and other insects that people consider to be pests.

Insects

There are millions of kinds of insects in the world. More than 90 percent of the animals on Earth belong to the insect kingdom. All insects have the following:

- six legs
- three body parts:
  head, thorax, and abdomen.

Citrus root weevil   Bombardier Beetle

Some insects, like bees, help pollinate flowers and fruit trees.

Some insects, like bees and ants, live in colonies and work together. There are over 10,000 species of ants.

You might like to start an insect collection. You can catch insects or draw pictures of ones you see. Keep a list of insects you've met (like the grasshopper and the firefly below).

Materials Needed for #2:
Bible(s), pictures of various animals
Computer and Internet, optional

God created every living creature on Earth on Day Six. Scientists have named and classified over one and a half million animals, but there could be 5 to 10 million kinds of animals alive today. (Over half of these are types of insects.)

The Bible mentions different animals. What animals and insects do we find in the stories of Jesus when He was on Earth? (You may wish to look up some of the references given.)

ass/ donkey/ colt — Matthew 21:2–7, Mark 11:1, Luke 10:34, Luke 19:31, John 12:14–15
calf — Luke 15:23
cattle — (KJV) Matthew 22:4, (KJV) Luke 17:7 (NIV, NLT) John 2:14–15, (KJV) John 4:12
camel — Matthew 19:24
dog — Matthew 15:26, Luke 16:21
fox — Matthew 8:20, Luke 9:58
gnat — Matthew 23:24
goat — Matthew 25:32–33
locust — Matthew 3:4, Mark 1:6
moth — Luke 12:33, Matthew 6:19–20 (see photo)

lamb — (omitted in KJV) Mark 14:12, (KJV) Luke 3:3, Luke 10:3, (omitted in KJV) Luke 22:7, John 1:36

fox — Matthew 22:4, Luke 13:15, Luke 14:19, John 2:14–15 (cattle in NIV, NLT)
sheep — Matthew 9:36, Matthew 12:11–12, Matthew 19:12–13, Luke 2:8, Luke 15,:4–6, John 10:2–4
serpent/ snake/ viper — Matthew 7:10, Luke 10:19, Luke 11:11, John 3:14
swine/ pig — Matthew 8:30, Mark 5:11, Luke 15:15
wolf — Matthew 10:16, John 10:12 (see photo)

Other animals found in the Bible include:

ape — 1 Kings 10:22
bear — 1 Samuel 17:37, Proverbs 17:12, Isaiah 11:7, Isaiah 59:11
chameleon — (see photo) Leviticus 11:30
deer — Deuteronomy 12:15, 2 Samuel 22:34, Psalm 18:33, 42:1, 1 Chronicles 12:8, Job 39:1,
dromedaries — 1 Kings 4:28, Esther 8:10, Isaiah 60:6
greyhound — Proverbs 30:31
hare (rabbit) — Deuteronomy 14:7 (see photo)
horse — Exodus 15:1, Deuteronomy 17:16, Esther 6:8–9, Job 39:19, Psalm 33:17, James 3:3

Science Scene 2, continued

leopard — Song of Solomon 4:8, Isaiah 11:6, Jeremiah 5:6, Jeremiah 13:23, Habakkuk 1:8

lion — Genesis 49:9, Numbers 24:9, Judges 14:5–6, Psalm 34:10, Proverbs 30:30, Daniel 6:22

lizard — Leviticus 11:29–30

mouse — Isaiah 66:17

mule — Genesis 36:24, 2 Samuel 13:29, 1 Kings 1:33, Psalm 32:9

weasel — Leviticus 11:29

MAMMALS:

When people hear the word animal, they often think of mammals. (Cats, monkeys, foxes, cows, horses, lions, etc.)

All mammals have these basic characteristics:

A mammal has fur or hair.

A mammal has a backbone.

A mammal is warm–blooded.

A mammal has four limbs (legs, arms)

A mammal breathes air through its lungs.

A mammal baby drinks milk from its mother.

Most mammals are born alive (rather than hatch from eggs). There are approximately 5,400 species of mammals.

Discover more exciting facts about animals and insects, their habits and habitats; and enjoy interesting mammal images, posters, and coloring pages:

www.masterbooks.org

Art Activity

Materials Needed:

Paper

Tempera paint

- Fold a piece of heavy paper in half to divide it down the middle.

- Using the folded edge as the bottom, paint a design.

- While the paint is still wet, carefully fold the plain side against the painted side.

- Press gently to transfer the design to the other side.

- Open the paper and lay it flat to dry.

You have created a symmetric design!

Examples of symmetry:

Extra Activity

Materials Needed:

Paper

Tempera paint or markers

- Fold a plain piece of paper in half the long way, then open and lay it flat.

- On the folded line, print or write your name.

- On the other side of the line, copy the letters of your name so they form a mirror image.

- Decorate your symmetrical name picture — keeping both sides the same.

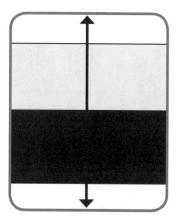

Spelling Spree

Honey Bee:

Materials Needed:
Paper and pencil
Graph paper
Scissors

Choose words appropriate for the child's grade level/ability from this Creation lesson. (This can be done by the teacher or with the child.) Examples: animal, insect, home, habitat, sixth, mammal, symmetry, etc.

Have child read the list to you, pronouncing each word correctly and spelling it aloud. Make sure child knows the meaning of each word.

1. Have child arrange the words in the list from the shortest to the longest.

2. Look at the number of letters in each word and whether the letters are short or tall to help determine shorter and longer.

3. Write each word on graph paper, using one square for a short letter and two squares for a long letter (like f or g).

4. Cut out the words along the grid lines.

5. Trace each shape on a piece of paper.

6. Have child fill in the spelling words that fit each shape.

Give a spelling test at the end of the week.

Slug

Conclusion

Materials Needed:
Bible
The Creation Story for Children (optional)

To incorporate *The Creation Story for Children*, review the first half of the account of Day Six, with special emphasis on man and woman not being created just yet.

God told people to rule over animals.

God told people to take care of the animals.

How can we help take care of God's animals?

What things can you do at home, in your city, in the world to help care for various animals?

What are your favorite animals? What animals would you like to have as pets? Why?

Now let's thank God for all the wonderful gifts of animals we enjoy.

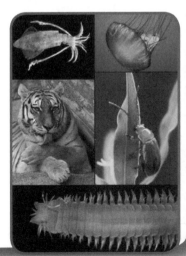

9 Lesson

Materials Needed:
Bible(s)
Fruit in a bowl

For Optional Activity:
Paper and pencil

Kindness

When God gave humans rule over the animals, He wanted them to be kind to all His creatures.

God also tells people to be kind to each other. ("Be kind to one another . . ." Ephesians 4:32.)

Kindness is catching. One kind act sparks another.

The Golden Rule:
   "Do unto others as you would have them do unto you."

Jesus said to treat other people as you want to be treated. (Read Matthew 7:12.)

Why do you suppose this is called "The Golden Rule"? (Discuss.)

Character Connection

What do kind people do?
- **Kind people are sensitive to other's feelings.**

- **Kind people are good listeners.**

- **Kind people show they care about others.**

- **Kind people are friendly.**

- **Kind people are helpful to others.**

- **Kind people think about how their actions or words will affect others.**

Share some examples of kindness.
(Encourage personal sharing.)

How do you feel when you are treated kindly? (Encourage personal sharing.)

Scripture Search
Proverbs 17:17	Proverbs 31:20
Ecclesiastes 4:9–10	Romans 12:10
1 Corinthians 13:4–7	Ephesians 4:32
Colossians 3:12	2 Peter 1:5-7

Have you heard of "random acts of kindness"?

This is when people do kind things for others, even for people they may not know.

Think of at least three ways you can do unexpected kind acts for others and make the world the better place.

Optional Activity

Create a list of **ABCs of kindness.**

Think of **a verb** and **a noun** for as many letters of the alphabet as you can.

For example:
   I **a**sked for an **a**pple for **A**nna.
   I **b**uttered **b**read for the **b**aby.

You might want to draw pictures to go along with each of these.

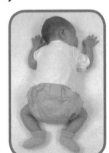

For Closing Discussion:

Kindness is a "fruit of the spirit."

Read Galatians 5:22–23. (Kindness is called gentleness in the King James version.)

Write down the nine fruits in this list.

How do these nine kinds of fruit work together? (Discuss.)

In what way will you show kindness today?

KINDNESS Reminder:

Place a bowl of fruit on the table.

When you see or eat a piece of fruit, think about the fruit of kindness.

Plan a random act of kindness you will do for someone in your family.

All kinds of people can be kind.

Lesson 10

God Creates People

"The LORD God formed man of the dust of the ground, and breathed into his nostrils the breath of life; and man became a living soul . . . And the rib, which the LORD God had taken from man, made he a woman" (Genesis 2:7, 22 KJV).

Materials Needed:

☐ **INTRODUCTION:** Bible(s)
☐ **OBJECT LESSON:**
Long piece of paper about 6" wide
fan–folded into at least six sections
Scissors
☐ **MATH CONNECTION**
Pencil and paper
Computer and Internet, optional
☐ **ENGLISH/WORD WORK**
Paper and pencil
☐ **SCIENCE SCENE**
Pictures of the parts of the human body (in an encyclopedia, etc.)
Computer and Internet, optional
Bible(s)
☐ **ART ACTIVITY**
Long sheet of paper—longer than the child is tall
Pencil, plus markers or crayons
Computer and Internet, optional
☐ **SPELLING SPREE**
Paper and pencil
Computer and Internet, optional
☐ **CONCLUSION:**
Bible, *The Creation Story for Children* book (optional)

Lesson Introduction

Materials Needed:
Read Genesis 1:26–27, 31
and Genesis 2:7, 18, 21–22.
Discuss any unfamiliar words.

Today we come to the "crown" of Creation. On Day Six, God created people in His own image.

**People can think and talk and pray.
People have eternal souls.
God created people to enjoy His presence.
God created people to serve Him.
God wants us to live with Him forever.**

What were the names of the first man and woman? (Adam and Eve.)

Object Lesson

Materials Needed:
Long piece of paper about 6" wide fan-folded into at least six sections
Scissors

- While speaking, cut the shape of a person from the folded paper—leaving the hands and feet joined (so it will open as one long piece).

First, God created a man from the dust of the ground.
- Hold up the folded person shape.

**This man, Adam, was lonely since he was the only person on Earth.
So God put Adam to sleep.**

**While Adam slept, God took a rib bone from Adam's side.
From this rib, God formed a woman.**

- Open one fold to reveal two people joined hand to hand.

God gave the woman to Adam to be his wife. Adam named his wife Eve.

Later, God gave Adam and Eve some children.
- Continue to open the folds to another person as you name them until all show.

Explain:
**Adam and Eve named their sons Cain, Abel, and Seth.
Adam and Eve had many sons and daughters.
Adam and Eve also had many grandchildren and great-grandchildren.**

**Adam and Eve were the first parents.
All people come from Adam and Eve, including you and me.**

- You may want to help your child make a row of paper people too — perhaps representing your family.

- You could write a person's name on each shape of a person, including grandparents.

Math Connection

Materials Needed:
Pencil and paper
Computer and Internet, optional

How many created things have we learned about in these ten lessons about God's Creation?

Let's count and find the total.
   LIGHT + SKY + WATER + LAND + PLANTS + SUN + MOON + STARS + SEA CREATURES + BIRDS + ANIMALS + PEOPLE = [12].

Have child create word problems, with answers from one to ten. These can be as simple or difficult as the child is able to solve. Following are some examples to get you started.

1. **Adam and Eve had two sons. One son died, then another son was born. How many people were alive after the third son was born?**

   $2 + 2 (= 4) - 1 (= 3) + 1 = [4]$.
   (Child may be able to solve this mentally.)

2. **There were twelve apples on a tree. Abel picked three apples. How many apples were left on the tree?**
   $12 - 3 = [9]$.

3. **Seth picked four daisies, two tulips, and one rose for his mother. How many flowers were in his bouquet?**
   $4 + 2 + 1 = [7]$.

- Check the problems to make sure they are answered correctly.

- Share these word problems with friends or siblings for them to solve.

Find websites offering online math practice:

www.masterbooks.org

English Word Work

Materials Needed:
Paper and pencil

Today we will do a stretching exercise with sentences.
(This can be done orally or as a written exercise.)

Choose a noun and a verb to form a simple sentence.
Example: Adam ran.

Add another word to the sentence.
Example: Adam ran quickly (adverb added).

Keep adding words until you can't think of any other ways to stretch out your sentence.

Examples: Adam ran quickly to the river.
1. Adam ran quickly to the river to get water.

2. Adam ran quickly to the river to get water for Eve.

3. Adam ran quickly to the river to get water for Eve to wash.

4. Adam ran quickly to the river to get water for Eve to wash the vegetables.

5. Adam ran quickly to the river to get water for Eve to wash the vegetables she had picked that morning.

6. Adam ran quickly to the river to get water for Eve to wash the vegetables she had picked that morning for lunch.

7. Adam ran quickly to the river to get water for Eve to wash the vegetables she had picked that morning for lunch to feed the family.

8. One morning, Adam ran quickly to the river to get water for Eve to wash the vegetables she had picked that morning for lunch for the family.

9. One sunny morning, Adam ran quickly to the river to get water for Eve to wash the vegetables she had picked that morning for lunch for the family.

NOTE: You can go on and on, making as long a sentence as long as you want.

Do ten sentence stretches.
This can also be played as a game, taking turns adding words to the sentence.

Each player continues adding to the sentence until it no longer makes sense or a player forgets part of the sentence or puts the words in the wrong order.

Science Scene

Materials Needed:

Pictures of the parts of the human body (in an encyclopedia, etc.)
Computer and Internet, optional
Bible(s)

God made the human body wonderfully complex. Each part of the body shows it was specially designed.

Our great Creator made our eyes to see, our ears to hear, our tongues to taste, our noses to smell, our skin to feel, our minds to think, and so much more.

SKELETON:

A skeleton made up of bones supports the body.
The skeleton gives the body its shape.
The skeleton helps the body move.
Muscles attached to the bones make them move.
The skeleton also protects important body organs, like the heart and lungs and brain. (Help child find and feel the skeletal bones In his hand.)

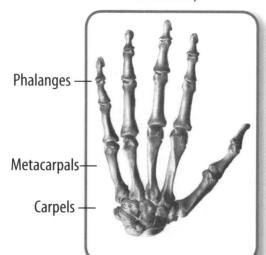

Phalanges

Metacarpals

Carpels

HEART and BLOOD:
The heart pumps blood through the body. Blood carries oxygen from the lungs throughout the body, from your head to your feet.

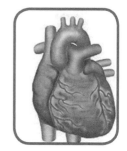

(Look for your blood vessels on your arm, leg, back of hand, etc. Can you feel your heart beat when you place a finger on your inner wrist or on the vein in your neck?)

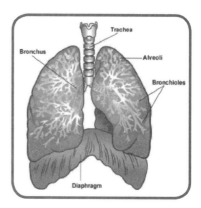

Trachea

Bronchus

Alveoli

Bronchioles

Diaphragm

LUNGS:
The lungs take the air you breathe and move oxygen into the blood vessels. The lungs also take the used-up air from the blood and breathes it out.
(Take deep breaths to feel the lungs move.)

What Does God Look Like?

In the Bible, God is described as having physical body parts, like humans. Even though God is a spirit, without a body, this imagery helps us to understand God better and picture God in our minds.

Here are Bible verses about some of God's features:

God's heart — Genesis 8:21, 1 Samuel 13:14, Psalm 33:11

God's shoulder — Isaiah 9:6

God's arms — Deuteronomy 9:29, Isaiah 51:5, Deuteronomy 33:27, Jeremiah 32:17

God's hand — Deuteronomy 3:24, Joshua 4:24, Nehemiah 2:18, Job 27:11, Psalm 48:10, Psalm 98:1, Isaiah 41:10

God's feet — Exodus 24:10, Isaiah 66:1, Nahum 1:3

God's face — Genesis 32:30, 2 Chronicles 6:42, Psalm 17:15, Psalm 27:8, Psalm 67:1

God's eyes — 2 Chronicles 16:9, Psalm 11:4, Psalm 34:15, Psalm 139:16, Jeremiah 32:19

God's ears — 2 Samuel 22:7, Isaiah 59:1, 1 Peter 3:12

God's mouth — Numbers 12:8, Isaiah 40:5, Deuteronomy 8:3, 1 Kings 8:15

God's voice — Genesis 3:8, Job 40:9, Psalm 29:3-9, Isaiah 30:30

What did Jesus say about God?:

Jesus said, "God is Spirit, and those who worship Him must worship in spirit and truth" (John 4:24 KJV).

Jesus said that anyone who knew Him also knew His Father (John 14:7).

Jesus told His disciples that if they had seen Him, they had seen His Father (John 14:9).

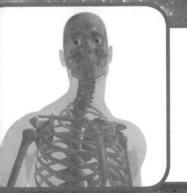

Visit this link to view a website containing information and printable worksheets about the human body and its parts:

www.masterbooks.org

Art Activity

Materials Needed:
Long sheet of paper (make sure it is longer than the child is tall)
Pencil
Markers or crayons
Computer and Internet, optional

1. Have child lie on the paper and trace around the body, including each finger and the hair.

2. Child then fills in the features, creating a life–size self-portrait.

3. You may wish to take a photo of the child with his or her "twin" or have them stand "side-by–side" and look in the mirror to see how they match.

Remind your child:
You are the CROWN of God's creation! God made you a very special person!

Spelling Spree

Materials Needed:
Paper and pencil
Computer and Internet, optional

Choose words appropriate for the child's grade level/ability from this Creation lesson. (This can be done by the teacher or with the child.)

Examples: man, woman, people, person, Adam, Eve, heart, blood, lungs, bones, hand, skeleton, portrait, crown, special, etc.

Have child read the list to you, pronouncing each word correctly and spelling it aloud. Make sure child knows the meaning of each word.

Give a spelling test on the words at the end of the week.

(See next page for extra activity.)
Translate the spelling words into Morse Code, a system of dots and dashes that stand for letters.

Ready for some more challenges? Try making a fabric self-portrait, or have fun online with a Morse Code translator:

www.masterbooks.org

A	.-	G	--.	M	.-..	S	...	Y	-.--
B	-...	H	--.	N	-.	T	-	Z	--..
C	-.-.	I	..	O	---	U	..-		
D	-..	J	.---	P	.--.	V	...-		
E	.	K	-.-	Q	--.-	W	.--		
F	..-.	L	.-..	R	.-.	X	-..-		

Conclusion

Optional Activities with the MORSE CODE:

- You can also listen to the sound version of Morse Code at the website on the facing page.

- You might try a spelling quiz with the sounds.

- Perhaps you will want to memorize Morse Code and use it.

- Either have child write the words in Morse Code or decipher them from the list you translate.

Materials Needed:
Bible (Psalm 139)
The Creation Story for Children (optional)

On Day Six, God completed His marvelous creation when He created the first man and woman.

Read Psalm 139. God also created you and me. Psalm 139 tells how God knows every person and sees them wherever they are. God is always with us, watching over us.

Verse 13 says God formed each of us inside our mother's body.
Verse 14 reminds us we are wonderfully made by our Creator.

Think about what you have learned about some of the parts of your body. What is special about your eyes, ears, hands, heart, and brain? (Talk about the intricacies of various body parts and how they all work together. Do further research or look at the websites listed on page 6.)

God recorded all the days of our lives before we were even born (Psalm 139:16). **Doesn't that make you feel special? God loves you so much! Let's praise God for all He has made, including us.**

Respect

Materials Needed:
Bible(s)
Craft sticks and marker

For Optional Activity:
Card stock, markers, rubber stamps, stickers, etc., to make cards.

Why should being created in God's own image make us respect each other? (Discuss.)

We should also respect our bodies and take good care of them. What are some ways we can do this? (Eating healthy food, getting enough sleep, exercise, washing, drinking water, etc.)

When we respect others, we treat them well and talk nicely to them.

- **Respectful people don't just think about themselves. They act for the good of others.**

- **Respectful people are polite and use good manners.**

Character Connection

What do respectful people do?

- **Respectful people follow the rules.**

- **Respectful people don't look down on others.**

- **Respectful people don't yell at others, or say bad things about them, or laugh at them.**

- **Respectful people control their tone of voice as well as their words.** (demonstrate)

- **We should especially respect older people, our parents, teachers, pastors, government leaders, and all those who are in charge.**

Scripture Search
Exodus 20:12   Leviticus 19:32;
Proverbs 23:22   Romans 13:1
Colossians 4:6   1 Timothy 5:1-3
1 Peter 2:17–18   1 Peter 3:8-11
1 Thessalonians 5:11–15

How can you show respect for your neighbors? (Encourage personal sharing.)

How can you show respect for your pastor? (Encourage personal sharing.)

How can you show respect for your family? (Encourage personal sharing.)

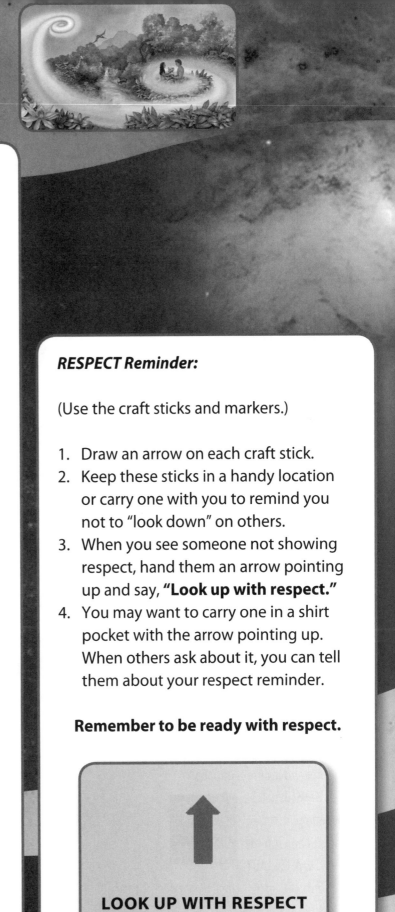

Optional Activity

Make cards to tell others you respect them.

1. Decorate the front however you want.

2. Inside write a message of your own about respect or use this one:

   > I just want to tell you that you are special and I respect you.

3. Be sure to sign your name.

4. You might give them to a teacher, pastor, policeman, or other person in leadership.

For Closing Discussion:

How do you feel when people don't show respect to you? (Encourage personal sharing.)

How can we show respect even to those who are not nice to us?

How do we show we respect God?

In what ways will you be respectful today to other children? . . . to adults? . . . to senior citizens? . . . to our leaders? . . .to someone who is sick or handicapped? . . . to teachers?

Do you treat some people better than you do other people? (Read James 2:1–9.)

RESPECT Reminder:

(Use the craft sticks and markers.)

1. Draw an arrow on each craft stick.
2. Keep these sticks in a handy location or carry one with you to remind you not to "look down" on others.
3. When you see someone not showing respect, hand them an arrow pointing up and say, **"Look up with respect."**
4. You may want to carry one in a shirt pocket with the arrow pointing up. When others ask about it, you can tell them about your respect reminder.

Remember to be ready with respect.

↑

LOOK UP WITH RESPECT

God Creates a Day of Rest

"Thus the heavens and the earth were finished, and all the host of them. And on the seventh day God ended his work . . . and he rested on the seventh day from all his work . . . And God blessed the seventh day, and sanctified it: because that in it he had rested from all his work" (Genesis 2:1–3 KJV).

Materials Needed:

☐ **INTRODUCTION:** Bible(s)

☐ **OBJECT LESSON:**
The letters **A, D, E, R, S, T, Y** each written on separate pieces of paper

☐ **MATH CONNECTION**
Pencil and paper
Computer and Internet, optional

☐ **ENGLISH/WORD WORK**
Paper and pencil

☐ **SCIENCE SCENE**
Scale
Grocery items with weights listed on the label
Pencil and paper
Magnet and compass
Pins, paper clips, or other small metal objects
Computer and Internet, optional

☐ **ART ACTIVITY**
Paper
Ink pad or paint
Computer and Internet, optional

☐ **SPELLING SPREE**
Paper and pencil
Computer and Internet, optional

☐ **CONCLUSION:**
Bible, *The Creation Story for Children* book (optional)

Sabbath

Exodus 20:8 "Remember the sabbath day, to keep it holy."

Definition from Wikipedia:

The term "sabbath" comes from the Hebrew *shabbat*, "to cease," which was first used in the Biblical account of the seventh day of Creation. Observation and remembrance of the Sabbath is one of the Ten Commandments.

The Jewish Sabbath ("shabbat") is a weekly day of rest observed from sundown on Friday, when candles are lit in each home, until the appearance of three stars in the sky on Saturday night.

Lesson Introduction

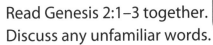

Materials Needed::
Bible(s)

Read Genesis 2:1–3 together.
Discuss any unfamiliar words.

On the seventh day, God rested from His work of Creation. God blessed this day and made it special.

God wants us to set aside one day each week to rest and to gather with other believers to worship Him.

**God set an example for us when He rested on this special day.
Isn't it interesting that God would stop to rest? Do you think God was "tired" after all the work of CREATION?** (No.)

Or did God want to help us enjoy His creation and not work all the time?

What is God's commandment about the "Sabbath" day of rest (Exodus 20:8–11)?

God wants us to spend time enjoying Him and each other on one special, re-laxing day.

Object Lesson

Materials Needed:
The letters A, D, E, R, S, T, Y each written on separate pieces of paper

Today we are studying Day Seven of Creation. Here are seven letters. Arrange them to form two words that tell what God intends this day to be.
(REST DAY)

What does it mean to rest? (Not to work, to sleep, to sit quietly, to relax, etc.)

What do you like to do to "relax"?

God wants us to rest from our regular work on His Day. This day is called the Lord's Day because it is a special day set aside each week to honor God.

Discuss and plan how you will make your next "Day of Rest" extra–special and an honor to God.
What can we do to "honor God" on the Lord's Day? What can we do to honor each other and bless each other?

How can we honor the Lord's Day?
(Worship God, sing, pray, read the Bible, visit other people, invite people to our home for fellowship, etc.)

Math Connection

Materials Needed:

Pencil and paper
Computer and Internet, optional

What do we call the number that stands for nothing? (0, zero)
When we add zero to another number does it change that number? (no)
Demonstrate: $1 + 0 = 1$. $10 + 0 = 10$.

When we subtract zero from another number does it change that number? (No.)
Demonstrate: $2 - 0 = 2$. $8 - 0 = 8$.

0

What if we add 0 + 0? (we get 0)
Nothing plus nothing is nothing.
Nothing minus nothing is still nothing.
Demonstrate: $0 – 0 = 0$.

Working with zero reminds me of resting. Adding or subtracting zero does not make work.
But zero does work too.
Zero can be a placeholder in a number.

We divide numbers greater than nine (9) into columns.
   The first column on the right is the ones column.
   The column to the left of the ones column is the tens column.
   The column to the left of the tens column is the hundreds column.

The column to the left of the hundreds column is the thousands column.
[The number 1,230 is read 1 (one thousand), 2 (two hundred) 3 (thirty) 0.]
In the number 10, the zero shows us there are no numbers in the ones column.
The zero holds the place for the ones column since it is empty.

In the number 100, the zeros show us there are no numbers in the ones column or in the tens column.
The zero holds the place for the tens column and the ones column since they are empty.

Which columns are empty in these numbers?
>   205 (tens column)
>   7,012 (hundreds column)
>   503 (tens column)
>   980 (ones column)
>   40 (ones column)
>   1,010 (hundreds column)
>   600 (tens and hundreds columns)
>   3,000 (ones, tens, and hundreds
>   columns)

For more practice:
Have child write numbers with zero as a placeholder in each column you call out.
Add and subtract numbers with zeros.

English Word Work

Materials Needed:
Paper and pencil

A word that reads the same forward or backward is called a palindrome [pal-in-drohm].
Read these words from left to right.

dad	bib	gag	pop
mom	pep	pup	did
eye	radar	rotor	solos
wow	racecar	madam	yay

Then read the same words from right to left. They're the same both ways.

Even names can be palindromes, like Eve, Anna, and Hannah.

Palindromes can also contain more than one word.

Read these from left to right and right to left:

> Not a ton
> Never odd or even
> No lemon, no melon
> Stop pots
> Start tarts

Palindromes can be sentences too.

> Too bad I hid a boot.
> Was it a car or a cat I saw?
> Dee saw a seed.
> Don did nod.
> No miss, it is Simon.
> Pull up.
> Step on no pets.
> We sew.

You can make more palindrome sentences by changing the cat in this sentence to other words that end with _at.

> Was it a cat I saw?

(C is the middle letter. Replace it with b, h, m, r, etc.)

Here's a riddle with a palindrome answer:
What *did* Adam say when he met *Eve*?
(There are two palindromes in this question—the words in Italics.)

> Answer: "Madam, I'm Adam."

- Look for palindromes in other sentences.
- Make a list of palindromes you find or think of.
- Try to create your own palindrome sentence.

Materials Needed:

Scale, Grocery items with weights listed on label, pencil and paper, magnet
Pins, paper clips, other small metal objects
Compass
Computer and Internet, optional

A force is a push or a pull.

GRAVITY:
Gravity is a force that pulls down or holds things to the Earth.

Gravity pulls things toward the center of the Earth.
Gravity makes water run downhill.
Gravity makes a sled slide down a snowy slope.
The force of gravity also makes things have weight.

How much do you weigh?
Check weight on a scale.

We weigh things in pounds and ounces. One pound contains sixteen (16) ounces.

1. Look at different grocery items and read the weights on the label.
2. Have child arrange these in order of weight from the smallest to the largest.
3. Have child lift a light object in one hand and a heavy object in the other.

Can you feel the difference in weight?

• Now compare objects that are different shapes and sizes but weigh the same.

Would a one-pound bag of feathers be as heavy as a one-pound can of soup? (Yes.)

FRICTION:
Friction is a force that makes it harder to move things.
When things rub together they cause friction.

1. Rub your hands together back and forth very quickly.
   Can you feel the friction?

Friction often causes things to get warmer.
Did your hands heat up when you rubbed them? (Yes.)
That's why people often rub their arms when they feel cold.

2. Roll a pencil across the desk or table.
   A smooth surface helps the pencil roll easily. There is not much friction.

3. Roll the pencil across a piece of paper.
   Does the pencil roll as easily as across the desk/ table?
   Is there much friction?

Science Scene, continued

4. Now roll the pencil on a rug or a blanket.
   Does it roll easily across this surface? (No.)

- **Friction keeps the pencil from rolling easily across a rough surface.**

- **Friction slows things down. When you are riding your bike and want to stop, how can you use friction?** (Drag your feet on the ground or put on the brakes.)

- **The friction of dragging your feet on the ground or pressing on the brakes so the wheels no longer turn helps stop the bicycle.**

MAGNETISM:
Magnetism is another force.

A magnet is a piece of iron or steel that attracts or pulls another piece of iron or steel.

Demonstrate with a magnet.
- Spread out pins and/ or paper clips.
- Use a magnet to pick them up.

Car mechanics sometimes use a magnet at the end of a long tool to reach a screw in a tight spot.

How can the force of magnetism help us? (Discuss answers.)

NORTH POLE:
The Earth also has magnetism. Magnetism pulls in the direction of the North Pole. We can use a compass to show which direction is North.

- Demonstrate with a compass.
- Show how no matter which direction you hold the compass, the needle always points to the North.

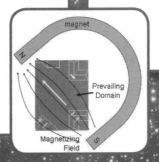

magnet

N

Prevailing
Domain

S

Magnetizing
Field

Find a great assortment of online math activities and math worksheets or websites offering information about compasses and magnetism:

www.masterbooks.org

Art Activity

Materials Needed:
Paper
Ink pad or paint of various colors
Markers
Computer and Internet, optional

Coat child's thumb/ fingertip with ink or paint to create fingerprint pictures. Markers can be used to add details, such as eyes and whiskers on an animal.

Create pictures of things God created. You can use this to make pictures on stationery, greeting cards, or gift tags too.

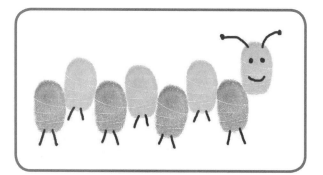

Spelling Spree

Materials Needed:
Paper and pencil
Alphabet noodles or Scrabble tiles

Choose words appropriate for the child's grade level/ability from this Creation lesson. (This can be done by the teacher or with the child.)
Examples: people, rest, work, seventh, commandment, gravity, friction, magnetism, etc.

Have child read the words to you, pronouncing each word correctly and spelling it aloud. Make sure child knows the meaning of each.

Have child use the letters from the noodles or the tiles to spell the words.

Child could try to form a crossword-puzzle style grouping of connected words.

Give a spelling test on the words at the end of the week.

Discover more ideas about fingerprint art, or watch a video online and see what may have been in God's thoughts as He rested after Creation:

www.masterbooks.org

Conclusion

Materials Needed:
Bible
The Creation Story for Children (optional)

The Creation Story for Children can be incorporated at this point by reading the account of Day Seven.

When God gave His people the Ten Commandments, He told them to set aside one day each week as a Day of Rest.

Names some reasons WHY you think you and I need to have times of rest and relaxation? (Need to take care of our bodies. Need time to talk to each other and have fun together. Need to take time to help other people, etc.)

What would happen if we worked all the time and never stopped to rest? Then people often experience "stress." What happens to you when you feel "stressed"?
(Stress can cause a lot of health problems. Stress and over-work can also cause people to get angry at each other and make more problems in a family.)

The fourth commandment says, "Remember the Sabbath day to keep it holy. You may work six days a week, but the seventh day is for the Lord your God.

On that day you shall not work, your children shall not work, your servants shall not work, and your animals shall not work.

It is a day of rest. For in six days God made Heaven and Earth, and on the seventh day He rested. So the Lord blessed the seventh day and made it holy."
(Exodus 20:8-11 paraphrased)

Can also read:
Exodus 23:12,
Leviticus 19:30,
Leviticus 23:3,
Deuteronomy 5:14,
and Hebrews 4:4.

Let's plan ahead of time how to make the Lord's Day a special day, a day of rest, a day set aside to honor God.

Lesson 11

Materials Needed:
Bible(s)
Paper and pencil

Optional Activity:
Red paper or white paper and red crayon
Black marker
Scissors

Obedience

God expects people to obey His commands.

God gave Moses the Ten Commandments, which list rules for right living. God said to rest on the Sabbath day.

God also put leaders, like parents and teachers, in charge, and we are to obey them.

What does it mean to obey? (Do what you're told to, follow rules, keep laws, etc.)

What happens when someone disobeys? (Discuss consequences, such as punishment, injury, guilt, etc.)

Character Connection

How does obedience make the world a better place? (Discuss.)
Why should we obey?
We should obey because we know it is the right thing to do, not just because we "have" to.

It is better to obey out of love than out of fear. Why? (Discuss.)

We should obey cheerfully because those who have rule over us are watching out for us, to keep us safe and well.

When we obey we make God happy.

Scripture Search
Exodus 19:5   Proverbs 1:8
Deuteronomy 26:16   Ecclesiastes 8:5
Romans 6:16   Romans 16:19
Ephesians 6:1–3   Philemon 1:21
Colossians 3:20–24   Titus 3:1

**The Bible says,
"Obedience is better than sacrifice"** (1 Samuel 15:22).

What do you think this means?
(Obeying is more important than putting money in the offering at church or giving food to the hungry, etc., although these are also important. Our obedience shows we trust God.)

Walk in OBEDIENCE

OPTIONAL Activity

Games require obedience.
What happens if we don't follow the rules? Without rules, the game won't go right. If we take turns and play correctly, the game will be fun for everyone.

1. Discuss the rules of familiar games, such as Mother May I?, Simon Says, tag, etc.
2. Play one or more games.
3. Be sure to obey the rules.

For Closing Discussion:

We find commands from God in the Bible and rules in all areas of life. Some rules are laws, like "Stop at a red light."

Other rules are for health, safety, etc., like "Wash your hands after using the bathroom" or "Look both ways before you cross the street."

List some rules for each of these. You may want to write them down.

      Home
      School
      Church
      Swimming Pool
      Highway

How will you practice obedience today?

OBEDIENCE Reminder:

1. **Cut an octagon from red paper or color one red (that was cut from white paper).**

2. **Write STOP in large letters across it.**

3. **Place this STOP sign where you will see it often.**

This sign will remind you to STOP when you're tempted to disobey. This sign is also a good reminder to STOP and take time to ask God to help you be obedient.

    To obey is the only way to go.

![Lesson 12]

Materials Needed:

☐ **INTRODUCTION:** Bible(s)
☐ **OBJECT LESSON:**
Bag to hold objects for each lesson.
Objects or pictures representing each
Creation lesson, such as: star, light bulb, bird, water,
fish, moon, leaf, stuffed animal, doll, dirt, sun, rock,
bee, flower

☐ **MATH CONNECTION**
Pencil and paper
Computer and Internet, optional

☐ **ENGLISH/WORD WORK**
Paper and pencil
Computer and Internet, optional

☐ **SCIENCE SCENE**
Paper and pencil
Things to taste: sweet, salty, sour, spicy
Magnifying glass and binoculars, optional
Computer and Internet, optional

☐ **ART ACTIVITY**
Shoebox or other small open box
Crayons or markers
Small toys, plants, pictures, etc., chosen by child
Computer and Internet, optional

☐ **SPELLING SPREE**
Paper and pencil, bowl

☐ **CONCLUSION:**
Bible, *The Creation Story for Children* book (optional)
Paper and crayons or markers

> *"God blessed them, and God said unto them, Be fruitful, and multiply, and replenish the earth"* (Genesis 1:28–29 KJV).

Lesson Introduction

Materials Needed
Bible(s)

Read Genesis 1:28–30 and 2:15 together.
Discuss any unfamiliar words.

God looked over all of His Creation and saw that it was very good. He had created a beautiful garden for Adam and Eve to live in, the Garden of Eden.

God gave Adam and Eve work to do, taking care of the Creation.
Adam and Eve were to tend the garden. God also made Adam and Eve rulers over all the animals.

Just as Adam and Eve were to care for God's Creation, so are we.

We should take good care of the Earth and the animals and the plants. We want to please God by caring for all He has made.

Object Lesson

Materials Needed
Bag to hold objects
Objects or pictures to represent
each lesson, such as:

> star, match or candle, bird,
> fish, moon, leaf, stuffed animal,
> dirt, rock, bee, flower, water, doll

NOTE: Put the objects in a bag so they can't be seen until the child pulls them out.

Tell child:

1. **Don't peek in the bag.**
2. **Stick your hand into the bag and pull out one object without looking.**
3. **Look at what you picked. Then tell me what part of Creation it represents and also on what day it was created.**

Let your child enjoy pulling out each of the objects one by one. Ask him what the object reminds him of and what day it was created.
(i.e., candle—light, Day 1)

Here are some examples:

> Star (sun, moon, stars)—Day 4
> Light bulb (Light)—Day 1
> Bird (Birds)—Day 5
> Cloud (cloud)—Day2
> Water (separates from land)—Day 3
> Fish (fish)—Day 5
> Moon (sun, moon, stars)—Day 4
> Leaf (plants)—Day 3
> Animal (animals)—Day 6
> Doll (people) —Day 6
> Dirt (land)—Day 3
> Rock (land)—Day 3
> Bee (animals)—Day 6
> Flower (plants)—Day 3

After talking about
all the objects,
lay the bag aside and
fold your hands and bow your head.

Then ask your child:
What day of Creation does this make you think of? (Day 7—God's Day of Rest)

Take time to thank God for His marvelous Creation we enjoy every day.

Math Connection

Materials Needed
Paper and pencil
Computer and Internet, optional

Ask your child:
Choose three numbers from 1 to 9. Write them at the top of a piece of paper.

Make as many two-digit numbers as you can from these three numbers.

For example, if you chose 1, 2, 3, you could make: 11, 12, 13, 21, 22, 23, 31, 32, and 33 (There are nine total possible with three different numbers used.).

Now write down as many three-digit numbers as you can.

(There are 27 possible combinations. For the digits 1, 2, and 3, you can make 111, 112, 113, 122, 123, 133, 211, and so on.)

How many numbers did you make from the three numbers you chose?

Make a chart of numbers from one to one hundred (1-100) with ten rows of ten, each row going across from left to right.

See how the numbers ending in one are in the first row going down, the twos in the second row down, etc.

You can use this chart to help you count by twos, threes, etc.

Continue your educational fun by counting sheep and divide them into the proper groups; or butterfly-themed activities to find missing numbers; or research a math glossary (illustrated dictionary) , arranged by grade level, or play a game practicing with odd and even numbers:

www.masterbooks.org

English Word Work

Materials Needed
Paper and pencil
Computer and Internet, optional

A homophone is a word that sounds like another word but has a different spelling and a different meaning.

What are three ways to spell the word that sounds like the number 2?
(two, to, too—these are homophones.)

What are three ways to spell the word by? (bye, buy, by)

- Make a list of homophones.

- Try to find a homophone beginning with each letter of the alphabet.

- Write a funny story using homophones or create some jokes or riddles.

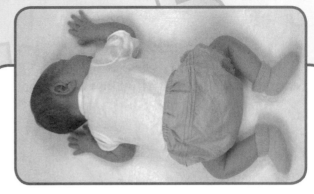

What's Your Name?

Materials Needed
Book of baby names and their meanings
Look up websites containing names and their meanings.

Suggestions:
Google: "baby names"
Google: "babys names world" for a site with 27,000 names

What is the meaning of your name?
What about your middle name?
In what way is the meaning of your name true for you?

- Look up names of other family members.
- Find out which were the most popular names given to new babies last year.

Read a list of common homophones:

www.masterbooks.org

Materials Needed
Paper and pencil
Things to smell (see list below) and taste:
(sweet, salty, sour, spicy, etc.)
Magnifying glass and binoculars, optional
Computer and Internet, optional

FIVE SENSES:
Humans have five senses.
Can you name our five senses?
(Seeing, hearing, smelling, tasting, and touching or feeling.)
We will use each of our senses today as we explore.

1. **Look around the room or out the window or go outdoors and list all the things you can SEE.**

2. **List all the things you can HEAR. It may help to close your eyes while you listen. Which sounds are quiet; which sounds are loud?**

3. **List the things you can SMELL. Sniff different objects** (Garlic, cinnamon, lemon, onion, chocolate, etc.). **Describe their odor. What smells do you like?**

4. **Let's TASTE different flavors. Close your eyes and stick out your tongue. I will put a bit of something on your tongue. Tell me how it tastes.**

(Note: Repeat for each flavor.)

5. **Our fifth sense is <u>TOUCH</u>. All of your skin can feel. Even your tongue and mouth have the sense of touch. You feel hot or cold, soft or rough. Now touch different objects and describe their texture.**

Not everything is safe to touch. Some things are sharp and may cut you.

What are some sharp things you need to be careful around? (Broken glass, knife, scissors, electric fan, drill, etc.)

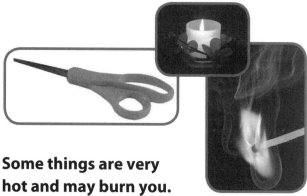

Some things are very hot and may burn you.
What things might be too hot to touch? (Stove, fire, matches, pan in oven, gas motors or electric motors, etc.)

We must be careful around sharp or hot objects and other dangerous things.

If you see something dangerous, always tell an adult.

God wants us to be safe and healthy.

Science Scene, continued

CELEBRATE FOOD TO EAT:
Eating proper foods helps keep our bodies healthy.

We need to eat a variety of food each day — fruits, vegetables, grains, dairy products, and meat or protein foods.

God created all kinds of good food for us to eat. God also gave us taste buds so we can enjoy eating!
Explore Nature

You may wish to take a Nature Walk and observe God's Creation and may collect samples, such as leaves, twigs, rocks, flowers, insects, etc.

Use your senses. Look, listen, smell, touch (carefully), and taste things that are safe to eat. Notice all the different colors.

Can you see the birds you hear calling?

Try lying on the ground to get a different perspective — first on your stomach, then on your back.

For each position, ask each other:
    What do you notice?
    What looks different from this view?

You could use a magnifying glass or binoculars in your investigations.

Get information on where you can find six different science games, or a website where students can find games, or others about eight different habitats, or more about the sense of touch or the sense of smell:

www.masterbooks.org

Art Activity

Materials Needed
Shoebox or other small open box
Crayons or markers
Small toys, plants, pictures, chosen by child
Computer and Internet, optional

Have child make a diorama to illustrate any part or day of Creation.

1. Begin by decorating the inside of the box. For example, you may want to color the sides and top blue and the bottom brown or green.

2. Pictures can be drawn or cut from magazines or found online and printed.

3. Arrange plants, animals, etc., in the box to show the scene.

Optional Activity:
1. Cut out pictures from greeting cards and magazines.

2. Make a picture book, gluing in the pictures.

3. Take the picture book to a nursing home and share it with people there.

Spelling Spree

Materials Needed:
Paper and pencil
Bowl

Choose words appropriate for the child's grade level/ability from this Creation lesson. (This can be done by the teacher or with the child.) Examples: creation, create, Creator, universe, senses, sight, sound, smell, taste, touch, feel.

Have child read the list to you, pronouncing each word correctly and spelling it aloud. Make sure child knows the meaning of each word.

1. Write each spelling word on a separate piece of paper.

2. Place the papers in a bowl.

3. Take turns drawing a paper and acting out the word for others to guess.

4. Have child spell the word aloud when it's guessed.

Give a spelling test on the words at the end of the week.

Visit this link for websites offering examples of diorama creations:

www.masterbooks.org

Conclusion

Materials Needed:
Bible
The Creation Story for Children (optional)
Paper and crayons or markers

Plan a Creation Celebration.

- Think of foods and games to represent the different days of God's Creation.

- Make invitations for your family or friends.

- You could have each guest design a special Creation Celebration place mat.

- You could sing songs together, praising God for His Creation.

- You could have people share about which item of God's Creation is most special to them.

- You may wish to take pictures of your Creation Celebration and make a scrap book.

If you chosen to incorporate The Creation Story for Children, re-read the book and do a final review on the days of the Creation Week.

Family Celebration

- Ask each family member to give a short performance (tell a joke, read a poem/ short story, sing or play an instrument, do a trick, or bring a "show-and-tell" to share).

- Encourage all to wear a costume.

1. Gather your family (and friends) together. Then explain: **"We are here to enjoy each other, to have a good time, and to celebrate each other and our great God!"**

2. READ: 1 Timothy 6:17
   How much has God given to us?
   (Lots!)
   What does God want us to do with all His gifts? (Enjoy them all!)

3. Celebrate and enjoy each other's gifts. Announce each person's act.
   Lead in cheers and applause after each performance.
   Give awards, high-fives, and hugs to each performer. Laugh a lot!

   May the celebration never end!

Lesson 12

Character Connection

Scripture Search

Psalm 92:1	Deuteronomy 8:10
Daniel 2:23	2 Corinthians 9:11–12, 15
Ephesians 5:20	Philippians 1:3, 4:6
Colossians 1:3	Colossians 3:15–17

Begin a list of things you are thankful for. Add to it throughout the day or week.

How do you feel when others don't appreciate you or the things you do?
(Encourage personal sharing.)

Gratitude is an attitude.

What kind of an attitude does God want us to have?

What is the opposite of gratitude?
(Fussing, whining, complaining, etc.)

We are to give thanks in all things. Read 1 Thessalonians 5:18.

Is it easy for you to give thanks for everything that happens to you? Why or why not?
(It is hard to give thanks in times of trouble, disappointment or when things go wrong.)

Who in the Bible had a good attitude about all that went wrong and caused suffering in his life?
(Joseph — Read Genesis 50:19–20. He knew his brothers wanted to hurt him, but God used it all for good.)

Materials Needed:
Bible(s)
Paper and pencil or markers
Note cards, optional

For Optional Activity:
Poster board, markers
Computer with Internet, optional

Thankfulness

Think about the wonders of God's Creation.
God planned this world to be a fine place for us to live.
How do you feel when you think about all God made?
(Hearts fill with thanks for everything.)

Why should we give God thanks?
(Discuss.)

Why should we offer thanks to other people? (Discuss.)

When we are thankful, we should let others know we appreciate the things they do, including God, of course.

Optional Activity

1. Make a poster expressing thankfulness to God.

Use flash cards (see link below) and/or draw pictures of things you are especially thankful for.

2. You could use the letters from the words **"THANK YOU"** and find something beginning with each letter.
   T = trees, tomatoes, taste buds
   H = home, heart, hamburgers
   A = apples, air, ants, avocados
   N = nose, nature, night
   K = kisses, knees, kites, kittens
   S = Savior, sunshine, strawberries,

3. Write a message of thanks to God on your poster.

For Closing Discussion:

**We often say thanks with words.
What are other ways we might show we are thankful to others?**
(smile, give a hug, write a note, offer to help with something, give a gift, etc.)

**Expressing thanks blesses both the giver and the receiver.
How will you show thankfulness today?**

THANKFULNESS Reminder:

Make some **"Thank Blanks."**

1. Write "Thank you for _____" on note cards or pieces of paper.

2. Carry some with you.

3. Whenever others do something kind or helpful, fill in what you're thanking them for and give it to them.

4. You can also thank God for each person.

When you pray throughout the day, remember to give THANKS.

Thank you for
_____

Print out your own flash cards related to the six days of Creation:

www.masterbooks.org

God's Great Plan for YOU

Lesson Introduction

Materials Needed: Bible(s)

God's work did not stop when He finished creating the universe. Each person in the world is specially created by God, our Heavenly Father.

God makes each baby boy or girl different from every other. God knows each one, and He has a special plan and purpose for every one.

God knows us before we are born. He sees us as we grow inside our mother's body.
Read Psalm 139:13-16.
What does verse 16 tell us about the days of our life? (God knows them before they happen!)

God calls people even before they are born.

Long ago, God told the prophet Jeremiah, "Before I formed you in your mother's body I chose you. Before you were born I set you apart to serve me" (Jeremiah 1:5 NIrV).

An angel announced God's plan for John the Baptist to his father Zechariah before the baby was formed.
Read Luke 1:13-17.
What would this baby be filled with even before his birth? (The Holy Spirit; see verse 15.)

God knows every detail of our lives from the beginning to the end. God also knows how He wants to use people to do His work in the world.

God works through people.
No one is too young or too old to be used by God. No one is too weak or too unimportant for God to use. Each person has a part in God's plan, including you.

God puts desires within each person. He gives everyone the abilities they need to fulfill these desires.

If we delight in God, He will give us the desires of our heart (Psalm 37:4).

The Bible shares stories about children used by God. We will look at four Bible children and how they served others and the Lord.

God had a plan and purpose for them, and God has a plan and purpose for you too.

God has placed you in your family, right where you are, right now. God wants to use you to be a blessing where you are.

God is also preparing you for the future — what you will do when you grow up and how He will use you in to be a blessing in the world.

"For I know the plans I have for you," declares the LORD, "plans to prosper you and not to harm you, plans to give you hope and a future" (Jeremiah 29:11 NIV).

God Uses Everyone

Questions for Discussion:

- **In what ways can I serve God today?**

- **How can I know God's plan for MY life right now? (Pray and ask God to show you what you should do right now. Read God's Word to find out what God wants you to do, etc.)**

- **What kind of an attitude do I have when others need my help?**

- **How willing am I to "give" to those in need (give money I earn, give my time, give my concern and care, etc.)**

Miriam

A Caring Sister
Exodus 2:1–10

Miriam was the oldest child of Amram and Jochebed. They were Hebrews (also called Jews), God's chosen people. Miriam had two younger brothers, Aaron and Moses. The Hebrew people were slaves in Egypt. Pharaoh, the king of Egypt, ordered all baby boys born to the Hebrew slaves to be drowned in the Nile River. He did not want them to grow up to fight against the Egyptians.

Miriam knew about this terrible order from Pharaoh. She helped her mother watch baby Moses and keep him quiet. They hid baby Moses for three months.

Miriam loved to take care of her baby brother. She enjoyed making him smile and watching him play. As Moses grew, he no longer wanted to lie quietly.

Their mother feared the baby would be found and killed. She decided to make a reed basket like a little boat, with a woven reed lid. Miriam helped her mother cover the basket with tar and pitch so it would not let in any water.

Mother fed Moses and rocked him to sleep. Then they put Moses into the basket and closed the lid. Mother pushed the basket out among the tall green reeds growing along the edge of the river.

Miriam said, "Shall I keep watch over little Moses? I can hide among the reeds."

Mother said, "Yes, you watch the basket with our baby and see what happens to him." Then Miriam's mother went back to her work.

Miriam crouched quietly among the reeds and watched the basket with her baby brother inside. The water gently rocked the basket bed.

The sun beat down on Miriam. She felt hot and itchy, but she did not leave her hideout. She must watch over baby Moses. She prayed for God to keep him safe.

Voices called to one another.

Someone was coming. Would they find the basket? What would they do when they saw the baby in it? Should she run to find Mother?

No, Miriam told Mother she would look out for Moses. She had helped care for him since he was born. She could not leave him now.

Miriam watched as an Egyptian princess came to the river with her maids. The princess wanted to cool off and wash in the river.

One of the maids pointed to the basket floating nearby.

"What is that?" asked the princess. "Go, bring it to me."

The maid carried the basket to the princess. Muffled sounds of crying came from the basket.

The princess slowly lifted the lid and looked inside. The baby stopped crying and looked into her eyes.

The princess smiled at the baby boy and picked him up. "He must be one of the Hebrew babies," she said.

"But, princess," said one of her maids, "Your father has ordered all their baby boys to be put to death."

"We will keep this one," said the princess. "I want him for my own son."

Miriam rose from her hiding place and ran to the princess. "Shall I find a Hebrew woman to nurse the baby for you?"

"Yes, go," said the princess.

Miriam brought her own mother to the princess.

The princess said, "Take this baby and nurse him for me. I will pay you."

So Miriam's family kept little Moses with them until he was old enough to live in the palace with Pharaoh's daughter.

Miriam still cared about her brother Moses even when he no longer lived in their home. She had helped save his life. She knew God had a special plan for him, and for her too.

Conclusion

Questions for Discussion

- **When you have a job to do, do you do it cheerfully or do you fuss and complain? Do you offer to help without being asked?**

- **How can you help care for younger brothers and sisters or other younger children?**

- **What are ways you can serve in your family right now?**

Choose one thing you can do to help out at home — something you don't already do.

Prayer

Dear Lord, please help me to show others I care about them. Let them see Your love through me as I serve them. Amen.

A Boy Who Listened

1 Samuel 1:11, 20-28; 2:18-21, 26; 3:1-11, 19

Samuel's mother, Hannah, did not have any children. She prayed to the Lord for a baby boy. Hannah promised God if He gave her a son she would give the boy back to the Lord.

God blessed Hannah with a baby boy. She named him Samuel, which means "Heard of God," because God heard and answered her prayer.
Samuel's parents dedicated him to the Lord, to serve God all the days of his life. When Samuel was still a young child, his parents took him to live with God's priest, Eli, and serve in the temple.

Every year when Samuel's family came to visit him, his mother brought a new coat she had made for him.

Eli taught young Samuel about the Lord God. Samuel loved the Lord and wanted to follow Him. Samuel helped Eli, who was growing very old. He worked in the temple and kept it clean and the lamps burning.

One night, when Samuel lay down to sleep, he heard someone call his name. "Samuel."

"Here I am." Samuel jumped out of bed and ran to Eli. "Here I am; for you called me."

Eli said, "I did not call you. Go back to bed."

Samuel lay back down. Soon he heard his name again. "Samuel." At once, Samuel jumped up and ran to Eli. "Here I am; for you did call me."

Eli answered, "I did not call you, my son, lie down again."

So Samuel went back to his bed and lay down to sleep. But once more the voice called out his name: "Samuel."

Again Samuel hurried to Eli. "Here I am; for you did call me."

Now Eli realized it was the Lord calling Samuel. So Eli told the boy, "Go, lie down. If the call comes again, say, 'Speak, Lord, for your servant hears.'"

Samuel did as Eli told him. As he lay on his bed, he waited to see if he would hear the voice again.

At last, he heard the voice call his name, "Samuel."

Samuel sat up in bed and answered, "Speak, for your servant hears."

Then the Lord told Samuel what He planned to do in Israel, and later, all that the Lord said did happen.

Samuel grew up to be a prophet of the Lord to the people of Israel. Samuel continued to listen to what God told him and then he passed God's messages on to the people.

Samuel became an important leader in the land of Israel. The Lord blessed Samuel and used him to help and to guide many people, including kings.

Two books of the Bible include many events in the life of Samuel:
I Samuel and 2 Samuel.

Conclusion

Questions for Discussion

- **How can you listen for God's voice? Does He speak out loud, or do you hear Him in your heart?**

- **What do you do when you "hear" God speaking to you?**

- **How can you prepare now to serve God in the future?**

Take time each day to listen to God in prayer. As you are quiet before Him, He will speak to you.

You may want to write down in a prayer journal what you hear Him say.

Prayer

Dear Lord, please speak to me and show me what you want me to do for You. Help me to plan and prepare to serve You in the way You want. Amen.

A Servant Girl

A Humble, Helpful Servant

2 Kings 5:1-14

Long ago, Captain Naaman led the Syrian army against Israel, God's special people. The Syrians invaded Israel and took captives.

One of the prisoners, a young girl, was given to Captain Naaman.

Naaman took the girl home with him. He gave her to his wife for a maid.

The servant girl worked hard in Naaman's home. When Naaman's wife told her to bring water or to clean up the room, the girl obeyed right away and did her very best.

The little maid knew God wanted her to help others and to serve wherever she was. Her Jewish parents had taught her to trust God. Her mother had trained her to work in the home, cooking and cleaning and doing whatever she was told.

Now the maid had been taken from her home. She had to work for people who were enemies of the Jews, but she still obeyed as she had been taught. She wanted to please Naaman's wife.

The girl put the wishes of Naaman and his wife ahead of her own wishes. Servants must always be ready to come when called, even if they don't feel like it. This little maid humbly worked in Naaman's home with a cheerful heart. She knew God was with her wherever she was and He would help her.

Captain Naaman was ill. His wife often cried, and the little maid could not cheer her up. Naaman had the terrible disease of leprosy. There was no cure! What would happen to Captain Naaman?

The girl remembered hearing about the miracles prophets had done in her homeland. God showed His power through these special men.

The maid said to her mistress, "Oh, if only my lord were with the prophet in Israel. The prophet would heal my lord's leprosy."

One of the other servants heard the maid say this. He went and told Captain Naaman what she had said.

Naaman thought if there was a chance he could be healed, he wanted to try it. So Naaman went to the king of Syria and told the king what the servant girl had said. The king sent Naaman to Israel. There, God used the prophet Elisha to heal Captain Naaman. But first Naaman had to humble himself and dip seven times in the dirty Jordan River.

Captain Naaman was healed from his leprosy. He now believed in the true God, the God of Israel. He returned home full of thanks and praise to God.

If this Jewish girl had not been a servant in Naaman's home, he would never have been healed or come to know God. Don't you think the young maid was glad God used her to help Captain Naaman? She, too, must have rejoiced and thanked God for the miracle of her master's healing.

Conclusion

Questions for Discussion

- **When have you had to wait for something you wanted and let others have their way instead?**

- **How do you act when others' ideas or desires are favored over yours?**

- **How can you show you are glad for others' joys and accomplishments?**

The next time others get chosen instead of you or win a game or an award, find ways to show you are happy for them and rejoice with them.

Prayer

Dear Lord, please help me not to want to put myself ahead of others. Help me to be humble and to be content to work with others and for others. Amen.

A Young Boy

A Boy Who Shared
John 6:1-14

"Mother, Jesus just crossed the Sea of Galilee and is heading for the mountains. People from all over are going out to see Him. May I go too?" asked a Jewish boy.

"Yes, you may go. I will pack a lunch for you." Mother gathered food and placed it in a cloth bag. "I know you will get hungry walking up the mountain. Be careful, and come home by dark."

"Thank you, Mother." The boy took the bag of food and a water skin and hurried after the group following Jesus.

He ran to catch up with some other boys he knew. The boys traveled with hundreds of other people who wanted to see Jesus.

"Maybe we will get to hear Jesus teach about God," said one.

"I want to see Jesus heal the sick," said another.

The boy nodded. He was so excited he almost dropped the bag with his lunch.

Jesus sat down with his disciples on the mountainside. All the people stood around them and listened to Jesus teach.

The boy and his friends stood near the front of the crowd, where they could see and hear everything going on. Listening to Jesus was so wonderful, the boy forgot about eating his lunch. He did not want to miss anything.

Later in the day, Jesus looked out over the thousands of people around Him. He said to His disciple Philip, "Where can we buy food for all these people to eat?"

Philip said, "Two hundred days' wages would not buy enough food for everyone to have a little."

The boy with the lunch looked into his bag. There were five small loaves of barley bread and two little dried fish. It would fill him up, but how could it help all the others?

I know, he thought, *I will give my lunch to Jesus. I can go home and eat tonight, but Jesus does not have a home or food here*.

The boy took his bag of food and gave it to Andrew, another of Jesus' disciples. Andrew carried the bag to Jesus.
"A boy here gave five loaves and two fish, but what are they among so many?"
Jesus told the people to sit down. He gave thanks to God for the bread and fish and gave the food to His disciples to hand out to the people.
The twelve disciples each carried a basket of bread and fish. Every time they reached into the basket for food, there was always more. Everyone ate as much as they wanted.
When the people were full, Jesus told His disciples to gather up the scraps so nothing would be wasted.

What do you think happened when the disciples gave back the boy's lunch bag? Perhaps, when the boy got his lunch bag back, it was filled with food. He had seen a great miracle that day. Jesus took his five little buns and two small fish and multiplied them to feed five thousand people. What a story he had to tell his mother! How his heart sang as he walked home carrying his bag of miracle food.

Conclusion

Questions for Discussion

- **Are you willing to share what you have even if it may mean giving up something you like or think you need?**

- **What are ways you can share your possessions or your time to help others?**

- **How do you feel when you give to others?**

Find a way to give something to someone in secret so only God knows what you did.

Prayer

Dear Lord, please help me to be thankful for what I have and happy to share with others. May I be a generous giver just like Jesus. Amen.

The Creation Story for Children

Enjoy a beautifully illustrated tour of the Creation week by David and Helen Haidle. From the first day when light was created to the final day of rest, the Haidles have designed a delightful book for young people to experience the wonders of our Creator's hands.

With richly-colored illustrations and easy to read text, the Creation story is shared in a visual treat for any reader!

Perfect as part of your education program or as a treasured gift, *The Creation Story for Children* also will be an incredible addition to your school, church, or home library. It is a book that children will enjoy over and over again!

Master Books®
A Division of New Leaf Publishing Group
www.masterbooks.net

ISBN-10:   0-89051-565-4
ISBN-13: 978-0-89051-565-5
$14.99
32 pages • 10 x 9
Available: August 2009